Parks for the People!
Profit, Power, and Frederick Law Olmsted in Louisville

Copyright © 2017 by Eric Burnette.

Direct all inquiries to:
Holland Brown Books, 2509 Portland Avenue, Louisville, KY 40212.

www.hollandbrownbooks.com

ISBN-13: 978-0-9897544-5-3

Library of Congress: 2017933654

Printed in the USA

FOREWORD

LOUISVILLE'S GREATEST NATURAL ASSET

Eric Burnette's current *Parks for the People!* is a welcome opportunity to learn about the wonderful Olmsted Parks and Parkways which we — park users and scholars alike — refer to as "Louisville's Greatest Natural Asset."

Frederick Law Olmsted was invited to Louisville in 1891 by the Board of Park Commissioners to fulfill their vision of three parks located throughout the City. Olmsted worked his magic with that notion and created three distinct, very different flagship parks – Iroquois, Shawnee and Cherokee. He took that vision a step further, and connected these three flagship parks with a system of Grand Parkways, wide tree-lined boulevards, that provided access from neighborhoods throughout the city. This system of parks and parkways is a unique gift that we have here in Louisville. In fact, Louisville is one of only four cities in the world that has a system of parks and parkways designed by Frederick Law Olmsted… one of only four!

Olmsted's sons, Frederick Law Olmsted, Jr. and John Charles Olmsted, and their firm continued to work in Louisville through the 1950s. We are fortunate to have a total of 18 Olmsted-designed parks and 6 parkways in Metro Louisville. Our Olmsted-designed park system is listed on the National Register of Historic Places. It was his last major parks work and is recognized as the culmination of all he had learned over the decades about fine and functional park design.

In addition to our parks system, the Olmsted firm lent their expertise to numerous private and public landscape projects throughout the city, including the subdivisions of Indian Hills, Cherokee Gardens, Iroquois Gardens, Audubon Park, the village of Anchorage, several campuses including the University of Louisville, and many private estates and homesteads.

Louisville's Olmsted parks define our city's character, strengthening our neighborhoods and the larger community. They return to the City and its residents a wealth of benefits: they protect us from environmental damage, provide opportunities for economic development, enhance our quality of life, and are magnets for recreation, relaxation, and physical and mental health.

They also improve property values and enhance tourism. It's hard to imagine Louisville without our beloved parks.

Olmsted Parks Conservancy, a non-profit organization founded in 1989, considers it an honor and privilege to help keep Louisville's greatest natural asset alive and essential to the community. Founded in response to citizens' calls to address significant park degradation in the mid-20th century, the Conservancy works to restore, enhance and forever protect the Olmsted-designed parks and parkways, connecting nature to neighborhood while strengthening our community's well-being. Since its inception, the Conservancy has worked with the community to raise some 35 million dollars in private funds to augment Metro Louisville Parks and Recreation's essential work, with the sole purpose of ensuring the Olmsted Parks System remains Louisville's greatest natural asset.

Olmsted Parks Conservancy
February 2017
www.olmstedparks.org

18 Olmsted Parks
Algonquin
Baxter
Bingham
*Boone Square**
Central
*Cherokee**
Chickasaw
Churchill
Elliot
*Iroquois**
Seneca
*Shawnee**
Shelby
Stansbury
Tyler
Victory
Wayside
Willow

6 Olmsted Parkways
Algonquin
Cherokee
Eastern
Northwestern
*Southern**
Southwestern

Designed before Frederick Law Olmsted's retirement in 1895.

Prologue

Slipping through the gate into Cherokee Park is like passing through an enchanted wardrobe or a magic portal.

The gate stands at the end of a road, across the street from a few blocks of stately Craftsmen and Colonial Revival houses—two square columns about six feet tall, chiseled at the top with fleurs-de-lis, the city symbol of Louisville. Judging from the wrought-iron stumps sticking out of the limestone, the actual gate part of the gate has been gone a long time. Only the columns remain; there is nothing now left to keep you out.

There are many entrances to Cherokee Park, and this is nowhere near the most obvious. It is an afterthought.

Frederick Law Olmsted had a genius for these kinds of afterthoughts, tossed-off entrances, sudden passages to other worlds, gates you wouldn't notice. One place would simply lead to the next, to the next, to the next… entrances everywhere, though you might never see them, or you might only see the first one. There will be a gate, then some trees, then a field, then some trees, and then…

Limestone canyons, limestone springs, light dancing under limestone ledges. The sound of water in the creek.

After a rain, you can't go thirty feet without running into water coming out of a rock, making its way to the creek, to the river, to the ocean.

We must be evolved to love that sound—for two million years, it was one of the happiest sounds you could hope to hear. It meant you would live. Even now, there is nothing like the sound of a gurgling stream to carry our troubles away.

A chorus of birdsong. Robins and cardinals, chickadees and gold finches, indigo buntings and yellow-rumped warblers. And pileated woodpeckers, which sound like monkeys or dolphins or something prehistoric but definitely not something that should be living in the middle of a city of a million people.

Beech trees that, in the fall, shine with the light of a hundred million copper leaves.

There is another entrance to Cherokee Park—more designed, more official. It begins with a bronze statue of General John Breckinridge Castleman mounted on a mare, looking down a tree-lined hill as if poised to invade. The road bottoms out in a little valley with a small playground, and then it climbs again and curves through the trees, and that's when you know you're in the park.

But even this entrance is indirect. There is nothing head-on.

It's not so different from Biltmore, really, which Olmsted also designed, with its grand, Spanish-tiled arch, promising an estate of great import and then…

You are embarked on a voyage through an ancient forest of oaks and conifers and tulip poplars, with splashes of azalea and rhododendron, until finally there is another gate, a formal gate, of wrought iron and gilded fleurs, and then a château falls on your periphery like a landslide. It is there all at once, in all its magnificence, leaving your stunned and breathless.

Olmsted had an affinity for the sideways.

When Olmsted was 28, he visited Birkenhead Park in Liverpool. He had never seen anything like it—a place of designed natural landscapes and planned moments of serendipity. The word "park" was not quite in his vocabulary, not in this sense, so he called Birkenhead a "garden."

Later, Olmsted would judge that the gate to Birkenhead Park was not right. It was too big, too showy: six pairs of Ionic columns, three arches, at a height of about thirty feet. Though he had been trained neither in architecture nor in what he would come to call "landscape architecture," he intuitively understood that the job of a gate was to telegraph what lay beyond it. This gate, Olmsted thought, was meant to impress. It suggested "a great display of art within."[1] And that is not what was within. To be sure, there *was* art within, but it was subtle. The gate overshadowed what lay beyond—the quiet beauty of nature shaped by design.[2]

There was another gate, this one made of "light iron." This one felt more honest, more appropriate. Olmsted passed through the second gate and was enraptured. He saw before him "a thick, luxuriant, and diversified garden." Never before had he seen art "employed to obtain from nature so much beauty."[3]

He walked along "winding paths, over acres and acres, with a constant varying surface, where on all sides were growing every variety of shrubs and flowers, with more than natural grace."[4]

After about a quarter mile, he came to a mowed field. There was a tent and some men and some boys playing cricket. There was a meadow, "with rich groups of trees, under which a flock of sheep were reposing, and girls and women with children were playing."[5]

It began to rain. Everyone took shelter under a pagoda, on an island accessed by a Chinese bridge.[6] Under the shelter, Olmsted saw that even in the midst of a class-obsessed Britain, the park was "enjoyed about equally by all classes… The poorest British peasant is as free to enjoy it in all its parts, as the British Queen."[7]

Birkenhead Park, Olmsted thought, was not unlike the New England countryside where he had roamed as a boy.[8] And yet, it was somehow better. It was nature, but deliberate. Improved. It was perfect.

Before he left, Olmsted quizzed the head gardener to get all the details of how they'd pulled this miracle off.[9]

If Olmsted really had his way, there would be no doors, no gates. Nature has many entrances but no gates. Gates are artifices.

The best entrances are the sly paths—narrow breaks in the trees, dirt slipping away into the shade. These entrances are the most honest. They telegraph exactly what you will find, if you seek it. They are the means and the end. Paths to peace of mind amidst the chaos of modern life.[10]

This is true now, just as it was in the 1880s.

CHAPTER 1

BLEAK TOWN

Louisville cradled the Ohio River like a fat banana. At each point, and at the bottom of the U, lay an "end"—East End, West End, South End (there was, essentially, no North End because the River cut the city off). Each of these Ends developed different neighborhoods, different characteristics, different histories.

But in the 1880s, they all shared an industrial squalor. Almost the entire town was the color of horse manure, which was abundant on the city's streets. The air, the roads, the buildings, all sickly sepia. One-hundred-sixty thousand people crammed into a dung-colored, dung-covered grid.

Smoke rose from every chimney on every house, every store, every riverboat. Coal ash sifted through the air, settling on roofs, walls, curtains, on furniture, on the cat's fur, on the children's hair. Inside, outside, dingy, pervasive coal ash carried its load of heavy metals and fine soot. People breathed it deep into their lungs, into their blood. It made them sick.

Evergreens couldn't survive downtown, though they were often planted. Coal soot and limestone dust combined to coat the needles in a noxious crust. Eventually the entire tree was fossilized in ash and cement. The ghostly mummified trees stood as testaments to one fact: the air was lethal. And unless people stopped burning coal or driving on limestone-Macadamized roads, it was hard to see how the air would become cleaner any time soon.[11]

The Industrial Revolution was a Coal Revolution, a Smoke and Smog

Revolution, a Pollution Revolution, and a Sick Revolution. Charles Dickens—who had been young when he visited Louisville in the 1840s—made a career writing about the coal fog that passed for air in Industrial England. "Smoke lowering down from chimney-pots, making a soft black drizzle with flakes of soot in it as big as full-grown snowflakes—gone into mourning, one might imagine, for the death of the sun."[12]

In *Bleak House,* as in life, coal set the scene for all that was to come.

There were so many ways to die from coal.

Men and boys dug into the black heart of Appalachia to bring it up, and not all of them made it back. In 1883, near Wilkes-Barre, Pennsylvania, six men were timbering a mineshaft 440 feet below the surface. When a 1,000-pound wood beam was being lowered, it knocked four of them off the platform, and they drowned in the twenty feet of water at the bottom. All had large families who were left destitute.[13] In East View, Kentucky, not six months later, a gas explosion killed seven men in a mine.[14] A little more than a year after that, again near Wilkes-Barre, a gas explosion killed twelve men. Seven of them left children behind.[15]

For those who escaped getting crushed or maimed in the process of mining or transporting coal, the possibility of death remained. For the miners, coal dust could turn their lungs black and become a disease, though they would not understand this for several more decades. In fact, black lung disease likely killed far more miners than mining accidents did.[16]

Coal floated down the rivers to Louisville, where was it was sold out of barges and coal yards and by coal dealers.[17] It came up the rail line from Jellico Mountain, near the Tennessee border, as fast as they could load it. Some of it stayed in Louisville, some kept going on the rails to other parts of the hinterland.[18]

Moving coal locally was still dangerous. In Louisville, a man named Michael Kennedy worked down at the rail yards on the Indiana side of the river. He shoveled coal into the coal cars of locomotives. A coal bucket fell and crushed his skull, "scattering his brains upon the platform." It took him several hours to die. He was 21.[19]

Coal carts were notorious for running people over in the streets as they took the fuel to its final destination.[20]

But, in fact, coal was most dangerous when burned. And it was burned all the time. Coal now powered nearly everything—factories, steamboats, trains, homes. It glowed in fireplaces, in stoves, in furnaces. It heated rooms and heated water. So necessary was it to every facet of contemporary life that "coal famine" was a genuine concern.[21]

As in London, Manchester, and Birmingham, the coal burned in the American cities west of the Appalachian Mountains was bituminous—the dirtier coal.[22] Coal fogs blocked the sunlight so completely that they could cause depression and bone-deteriorating rickets, as well as the obvious respiratory diseases.[23] In 1886 in nearby Cincinnati, some 31 percent of deaths were caused by respiratory illnesses, and tuberculosis, pneumonia, and bronchitis were the three leading causes.[24] When the *Louisville Times* claimed that "little ones" were "dying for pure oxygen," it was not hyperbole.[25]

Coal was a plague on all our houses; but it was a plague on some houses more than others. The rich could retreat to the country; the poor could not. Its effects fell most harshly on the children and the poor, and on poor children most of all.

In Louisville, "fresh air excursions" became a regular charitable enterprise, made possible by the Fresh Air Fund, the *Louisville Times*, and individual donors. At least one of the excursions was made possible, in part, by a donation from Andrew Cowan, a local leather merchant with a record as a war hero and the Yankee past of a perpetual outsider.[26]

On these excursions, poor families with children boarded boats and rode up and down the Ohio River. This fresher air—away from the city, but on a coal-burning steamboat nonetheless—was credited with a variety of health improvements.[27] There were even regular "orphan days." One such excursion featured a troop of orphans being marched down to the pier "in a soldier-like column." Once they were aboard, there was a rush of people trying to join them, many of them mothers with sickly infants, desperate for fresh air. The boat steamed down to a creek, where the crew gave a display drill of martial skill and handed out crackers to the great amusement of the orphans. All told, there were 178 nursing babies, 383 children, and 277 mothers with infants.[28] Healthy-looking girls and boys had also tried to get aboard, but guards kept them out. "The community ought to understand that these excursions are intended to benefit the sick children of the poorer classes, and not crowd the boat with well-to-do people," the *Courier-Journal* admonished. After all, as a means of providing fresh air, boats had their limits. Demand often exceeded capacity.[29]

That said, medical staff screened out those with contagious diseases.[30] It was a prudent measure, if a callous one. Dirty air was hardly the only public health problem facing urban America. A yellow fever epidemic, which began in New Orleans, had wracked the Southern U.S. in 1878, reportedly killing some 14,000 people, including at least 54 in Louisville, before it was stopped by a fortuitous hard frost.[31] A typhoid outbreak occurred in Louisville's Shippingport neighborhood in 1881, killing at least one and leaving other families in poverty as their breadwinners were incapacitated. It was blamed on the foul water of a low river and the swampy conditions of the neighborhood.[32] In the summer of 1883 alone, one death was caused by asthma, one by pneumonia, one by whooping cough, six by consumption; one by scarlet fever, one by diphtheria, one by malaria, two by typhoid, two by dysentery, six by infant cholera.[33]

Cholera was a constant worry since it had reached the United States in 1832 with devastating effect.[34] An 1873 outbreak of cholera killed 73 people in Nashville, but Louisville managed to escape a similar fate.[35]

Science, as it was, struggled to keep up with the causes of the disease.[36] Some understood that cholera spread along water routes. "The whole Mississippi and Ohio valleys may be invaded," warned the *Courier-Journal*. The paper also noted that the first victims of cholera "are the people of filthy habits and filthy surroundings, the poorly fed, the overworked," and recommended "cleanliness of person, of food, of houses, of back yards, of alleys, of streets, of vacant lots," as a means of combating the disease. "Thorough drainage, the removal of fœcal matter—these must be the rule at whatever cost," the paper advised.[37]

Indeed, sewage is one of the most fundamental challenges of any city. The easiest solution is to use a river or stream to carry it off. It becomes someone else's problem—someone downstream. But in the nineteenth century, American cities grew so rapidly as the population urbanized that streams and rivers simply didn't have the capacity to handle dense, urban effluent.[38] Little surprise that water was the common denominator for many contagious disease outbreaks.

Even the wealthy and powerful were not exempt from the consequences of poor sewage management. During the Civil War, President Lincoln's son Willie contracted typhoid fever and died. The White House drew its water from the Potomac River, and the tens of thousands of troops stationed in Washington to protect the capital had been using the river as a latrine. Water pollution was the proximate cause of Willie's death.[39]

When Charles Dickens disembarked at the Louisville wharf in 1842, Beargrass Creek would have greeted him as it emptied into the Ohio River, smack in the middle of downtown. The creek carried so much putrid offal, either from the slaughterhouses of Butchertown, or the sewage of eastern Louisville, that it was an economic blight. Dickens didn't remark on the creek; but he didn't stay long either. After spending a night at the original, lavish Galt House hotel and meeting a giant named Jim Porter at the Portland Wharf, Dickens caught one of the next steamboats down the river.[40]

By 1853, the city had decided to redirect the creek.[41] If it had to be such an assault to the senses, as least it could be an assault upstream. People needn't have to see it as soon as they got off the boat. Nevertheless, in 1866, the city's health office complained that Beargrass Creek still could still "'annoy the air' with [its] thousand stenches."[42]

Between 1840 and 1880, Louisville's population increased by 600 percent—from 21,000 to 123,000.[43] The sewage problem grew with the population. The old ways of maintenance, which never worked well, were now untenable.[44]

The streets were filthy, the air was filthy, the water was filthy, the people were diseased. And beyond all the cries for greater sanitation was something else, something no one seemed to name exactly, but which they seemed to feel, regardless of their backgrounds or races or money or political inclinations: the need to see something green, something alive, something soothing. For if you stayed in the modern, industrial city for too long, your soul would become calcified like the trees, and the grey dust would kill you just as assuredly.

And so came the Sanitary Reform Movement. Sanitary Reform promoted more air, more light, better drainage, better sewers, better water, less crowding, more parks, and more trees.[45] It was a *cri de coeur* for the soul to be put back into the city.

The movement gained traction: Cities built waterworks to import more reliably fresh water and sewage systems to dispose of the results.[46] Crowded tenements were opened up to allow better air circulation.[47] Cities established urban parks— parks big enough to forget you were surrounded by multitudes of people in a manure-hued, coal-hazed labyrinth.

The first such park was in Manhattan—the heart of the busiest, noisiest, dirtiest, most exciting city in the United States of America. Central Park was designed in 1858 by architect Calvert Vaux and a 36-year-old former farmer, former journalist, former sailor named Frederick Law Olmsted. Their plan, which had won a national contest, covered an astonishing 843 acres, at a time when most city parks spanned fewer than ten.[48] It was a park big enough to provide escape, even in New York. And if you could get away from New York in the middle of New York, you could get away anywhere.

As an offshoot of the Sanitary Reform Movement, the "suburb" was developed—a kind of park-neighborhood with wide, spacious lawns and air and light on all sides of the house. It provided a counterexample to cramped city tenements. The prototypical suburb was a Chicago development called Riverside.[49] It was also designed by Frederick Law Olmsted.

The city of Buffalo combined these concepts—the suburb and the park—to create a connected suburban park system.[50] They hired Frederick Law Olmsted to design it.

These new parks and garden suburbs were like lungs, allowing city people—common people—to breathe. And there was only one choice for a city looking to break through the industrial haze.

In the span of a decade, Frederick Law Olmsted went from being hapless young man, bouncing around from job to job, to being the only landscape architect anyone in the U.S. could name. He was the man every city wanted.

Despite having followed many of the Sanitary Reform trends—new water-works by 1860,[51] new sewers by 1868,[52] and new suburbs by 1872[53]—Louisville had been slow to catch up on parks. As late as 1881, Mayor John Baxter was complaining, "there is not a city in the United States even half our size which does not possess a public park."[54]

Not that there hadn't been attempts. There had been small parks here and there. There had been plans for the waterworks (thought of as both an engineering marvel and a scenic series of fountains and pools) to serve as a park. There was even a "Southern Park," designed by Benjamin Grove in 1860, but its utility as a public park was limited by the fact that it served as the grounds for the House of Refuge, which took priority. Eventually the House of Refuge was moved and the park abandoned.[55]

No, ultimately there were no real parks. Instead, Louisville had a random collection of make-dos.

There was Preston Woods, an undeveloped 30-acre triangle, atop a hill overlooking downtown. Preston Woods was park-like in some ways but also had a seedier reputation as a place where men, women, and boys would go to drink and carouse.[56]

There was also Cave Hill Cemetery, which lay across the street from Preston Woods. It had layers, hills, vistas, a lake. It had a wide variety of trees—canopy trees, ornamental trees, evergreens. It had songbirds and raptors and waterfowl. And it had hundreds and hundreds of graves. It was a park for the living and a city of the dead.

There were a few amusement parks, called "pleasure gardens." They could be lovely. At Woodland Garden, for example, gas lanterns lit the trees into a glowing wooded wonderland. But at the pleasure gardens, the beauty of nature was but one of many entertainments. They also had a carnival element, such as the black woman who claimed to be 127 years old and to have been George Washington's nurse (she was neither, but was later recruited for the circus by P.T. Barnum).[57] These parks were also private, exclusive, and profiteering.[58] They were not public. In Louisville, if the working masses wanted reprieve from the summer heat and the lethal air, they could choose only between the dead or the debauched.

This is the story of how that changed. It's a story of politics as much as parks, and avarice as much as artistry.

And it all began with a Scottish immigrant named Andrew Cowan.

Chapter 2

Two Yankees

Andrew Cowan was born in Ayrshire, Scotland in 1841. His family immigrated to New York when he was a boy.[59] If he retained any brogue later in life, those who worked with him did not mention it. His stereotypical dourness they did mention.[60] Even in college he had a stern countenance—thin lips, strong chin, and piercing eyes under a heavy brow and a swoop of brown hair.[61]

Andrew Cowan

The war erupted when he was a college senior. Cowan joined a New York infantry, and soon the Union Army.[62] After a year in the Army, Cowan was the captain of his own artillery battery. As long as he lived, Andrew Cowan would never see a place less like a park than his own battlefields. Men and trees and land, all fell under the thunder of his mighty cannons. Croplands burned in their fires. They—and their comrades and combatants—invented trench warfare. They obliterated everything they could find to obliterate, including 70,000 fellow men. All green beauty was blown to dust, everything but the instruments of destruction and the defenses against them—the cannons, the bunkers, the hills of dirt—these were all that was left.[63]

Having served the entire Civil War, including in some of its most important battles—Bull Run, Petersburg, Gettysburg[64]—Cowan became the definition of a carpetbagger, moving to Louisville to and making a fortune in the leather business.[65]

Cowan took a great interest in his adopted hometown and became a prominent citizen in its civic and charitable worlds. For an epochal 1896 history of Louisville, Cowan wrote an essay on the history of Louisville, beginning with its natural history. He wrote with the clichés of his time. He wrote: "The broad and fertile plain over which the present city is spread was then a virgin forest."[66] The white man's conquest became mythic, the rediscovery of Eden, Paradise Regained. And then it was lost, hacked to pieces with the iron axe.[67] "The mighty sycamores and giant oaks, the great beech and the lofty walnut trees, crowded upon the soil that was needed for sowing and planting, and were therefore but cumberers of the ground, to be cut down and destroyed."[68]

Well. He was right about that. They were destroyed. Almost all of them were destroyed. More woods were lost in the next fifty years than in the preceding 250.[69]

Before European logging, the trees of eastern North America grew to sizes not seen since. White pines in New England had measured upwards of 250 feet and hardwoods were fifteen feet around the base.[70] Then, beginning in 1850, deforestation went on a rampage in the United States. Losing these forests seemed to leave a mark of tragedy on the land—at least, that's how some of the Europeans saw it. How quickly they were losing any connection with the natural world! And not only would the great American forests be gone forever (apart from scattered sanctuaries, such as the redwoods and sequoias of the Pacific), but what had replaced them was so… ugly. For Cowan to have seen so much destruction in the war, and then to settle in *Louisville*, with its hazy, dank squalor, and coal ash mummifying the pines—it must have been depressing.

By his mid-fifties, Cowan had become an intense, stern, bull-walrus of a man with a handlebar moustache. Ever the man of action, when Cowan saw the need for parks, he resolved to do something about it. And so, years before Frederick Law Olmsted put drafting pencil to paper for the Louisville park system, Andrew Cowan was the one who envisioned the parks—how they should look, where they should be, what they should be, who should design them.

In 1887, Olmsted had maybe six or seven years left before senility. Details had begun to escape him. He couldn't remember whom he'd met with. He was overwhelmed with the workload of his firm and the demands on his time and energy. He was almost always in poor health. But his work was still of such striking beauty and simple power, he could not nearly be written off. In fact, Frederick Law Olmsted was peerless: there was none other like him; nor would there be again when he was gone.

Little about his early life could have predicted such success. Olmsted grew up in an upper-middle-class home in Hartford, Connecticut in the 1820s.[71] His mother died when he was three. He had seen her die, seen her overdose on laudanum, an opioid painkiller she took for her toothache—the kind of toothache he would later know all too well. Little Frederick ran out of the room screaming.[72]

And so began a long period of wandering. He wandered around the countryside because his stepmother didn't like him and didn't want him around.[73] He went from school to school and schoolmaster to schoolmaster, always the new kid, lonely, half-orphaned, lightly supervised, frequently disciplined.[74] He traversed the hills, "the uneven course of the purling brook, gliding among the fair granite rocks, & lisping over the pebbles; meandering through the lowly valley, under the sweeping willows, & the waving elms, where nought is heard save the indistinct clank of anvils & the distant roaring of water as it passes gracefully over the half natural dam…"[75]

Once, he wandered into a fateful patch of poison sumac, which gave him an eye infection so bad the doctors advised him to cut back on his studying. When it reoccurred a year later, they told him to give up on college.[76]

With college out of the picture, Olmsted wandered from job to job. He apprenticed as a surveyor but never became one.[77] He apprenticed to become an office clerk in the bustling, filthy New York of the 1840s, but the city made him homesick for the countryside, and he returned to Hartford after a year and a half.[78]

Then, quite literally reversing course, he signed up to be a merchant sailor and sailed to China. He got typhoid. He got scurvy. He got paralyzed, for a time, in his right arm. He barely saw the Chinese countryside.[79]

The voyage made him even more homesick. He returned to Connecticut and became a farmer, working a patch of land by the sea. Much of the horticultural and arboricultural knowledge he would later use as a landscape architect came from these farming years. He learned many useful things, such as how to grow plants in a nursery, how to construct drainage systems, how hemlocks looked in an ice storm—"they do appear magnificent," he wrote to a female friend. "Two of them (as I address you) have bowed their beautiful heads crown'd with fleecy light to the very ground… . how splendidly their dark green feathery spray, waving and trembling with its load of twinkling brilliants, shivers and glistens in the clear bright moonlight—like the green tresses of a mermaid toss'd in the foam of a breaking wave."[80]

Such pretty prose. Given his penchant for the romantic, it is no surprise young Olmsted fell in love. Indeed, he fell hard for the governor's daughter, Elizabeth Baldwin. They flirted for a while—long talks, carriage rides, reading Emerson and Lowell.[81] And then, remarkably, they were engaged. But Olmsted was in a prolonged adolescence, with no job, no prospects. He suffered from a series of fainting spells. He could not hold onto Elizabeth Baldwin, the "excellent princess," as he called her. She broke off the engagement.

In some ways, Olmsted would never let her go.[82] Baldwin was the last of his young loves. He didn't marry until his brother died and he took Mary, his brother's widow, as his own wife and her children—his niece and nephews, Charlotte, Owen, and John—as his own children.[83]

Somehow, this aimless, often difficult, early life resulted in Olmsted at age 35 being selected as the designer of Central Park in New York, along with Calvert Vaux, who would later become his first partner in practice.

Central Park was then the most ambitious public park in the United States—1,000 acres right down the spine of Manhattan. It was a triumph. For a debut, it was astounding. And it was followed by other masterpieces—Boston's Emerald Necklace, Prospect Park in Brooklyn, the US Capitol grounds, Mt Royal in Montreal, the campus of Stanford University.[84]

Within a decade, Olmsted became the only landscape architect anyone knew.

Yes, this was the man Andrew Cowan wanted for Louisville. But to get Olmsted, Cowan would first have to convince others in the city's old boy network of the need for parks.

It just so happened that Cowan belonged to a club comprised of some of these old boys. They called it "The Salmagundi Club."

And so Andrew Cowan invited The Salmagundi Club to a lavish dinner at his house on Fourth Avenue to talk about the need for parks in Louisville.

CHAPTER 3

THE SALMAGUNDI CLUB

The name, "The Salmagundi Club," was meant to connote a potpourri, a mixture of various ingredients, an eclectic group, which is not exactly how you might describe an exclusive, wealthy, white, male debating society, but the group's opinions, at least, could be diverse.

The Club had a flair for formality to the point of theatricality. They had a constitution, which stipulated the manner of their conduct to an oddly specific degree. Each member was to take turns hosting dinners, which were to take place twice a month. Constitutionally, supper was to be oysters "in one style or its equivalent," then meat with vegetables (the latter only if desired), followed by a salad (or its equivalent), followed by "an ice with plain cake," followed by coffee and cigars. Constitutionally, there were to be no flowers, fruits, or candles on the table, except at the Christmas meeting when candles were allowed. Later, the constitution was amended to allow candles at any time.[85]

Each Salmagundi meeting featured a conversation around one topic, led by two men, each of whom took opposing viewpoints and spoke for fifteen minutes. The rest of the members then each got five minutes to weigh in.

The Club covered topics ranging from municipal corporations to 18th century English novelists to whether Francis Bacon was the real Shakespeare.[86] Prefiguring similar debates more than 100 years later, they discussed the merits of classical versus scientific education, and "the effect of the concentration of

Wealth in individual hands in America, on our institutions—social and political."[87] There were also a fair number of racially themed topics, such as limiting suffrage in cities, "the Chinese question," "the Jew in History," and that sort of thing. "Whether slavery as practiced in the United States retarded or advanced civilization," sparked a lively debate, where according to member W.R. Belknap "the feeling was generally anti-slavery" but where Fontaine Fox, a lawyer, "distinguished himself for his strong Bourbon County slaveholding views".[88]

It was the Salmagundi Club that Cowan first sought to convince of his vision for a Louisville park system. If he was to succeed where others had failed, it would largely depend on this group of men. So Cowan tried to stack the discussion in his favor. He waited until it was his turn to host.[89] To avoid being the only face of the idea, he had Captain Thomas Speed—a fellow Republican, but a Louisville native—propose the public park system as an idea of his own.[90] Cowan might have been respected as a peer among Louisville's elite, but as a Yankee carpetbagger, he was better kept behind the scenes.[91] Besides, these park systems were a Northern innovation, and if someone were going to introduce a Yankee idea, it would be better for a local to do the introducing.

Speed began by reading a paper on the subject of public parks. When it came time for Cowan's five minutes of contribution, he backed Speed so persuasively that the Club gave him extended time.[92] Cowan proposed not one park, but three—one for each of the city's "Ends"—East, West, and South. And he was armed with examples, statistics, plans, and experiences from cities across the country.[93]

The Club loved the idea so much they created a committee, chaired by former Confederate major William Davis. The committee was to assemble a report. Naturally, they looked to Cowan to do most of the work. When Cowan read the committee's report to the full Club, every member endorsed it, which was remarkable, given the number of Confederates in the club and the egalitarian, vaguely subversive subtext of what Cowan was suggesting.[94]

The report was published as a Salmagundi Club op-ed in the *Courier-Journal* on June 5, 1887. "Parks for the People" was a 2,500-word essay, along with

rough map of the layout of each park, and a draft of a bill that would authorize the city to build and raise money for the parks.[95] It is an incredible piece
of public persuasion that runs the gamut from insult to flattery and includes,
at various points, appeals to pride, reason, equality, and, finally, self-interest:

Insult. Cowan began by going right to the city's insecurities. He said
it was "common opinion abroad that Louisville was a second-rate town…
of little importance"—that, in fact, even Louisville's own citizens bought
into this second-rate status. "We have been greatly prone to think that
other places were better than our town, other manufactures better than
similar goods made here; shops elsewhere superior to our shops; lands and
houses in our own city [as] investments to be shunned."[96]

Flattery. Cowan then reversed tack, writing that Louisville "boasted
of its geographical advantages as the gateway to the South; of its whisky
and tobacco as the best the world; its beautiful women; elegant homes,
and lovely cemetery, to which the visitor was usually driven as a part of
the regular entertainment of strangers."[97]

Pride. "It is time… for a general waking up," Cowan wrote. "If Louisville is indeed entering upon an era of great prosperity, we must learn to
pull together and help each other more than has been our habitat in the
past. We will have to put Louisville abreast of her sister cities in respect
to energetic action and vigorous self-assertion. We must have not only
employment for all who will make their homes among us… but we must
also provide for the recreation and health of the people."[98]

Public health. Cowan appealed to sanitary reform concerns. The city's
miserable air, full of limestone dust blew "in clouds through every window
or door that may be open…" Hundreds of children, he lamented, "perish
every year for lack of pure air and wholesome recreation."[99]

Equality. Louisville's many beautiful estates provided no relief from the
heat for "the largest part of our population [who] live from year to year in
small dwellings or rooms, oppressed throughout the long summer months
by the heat, from which they cannot escape."[100] In a strikingly class-based
appeal, Cowan wrote, "For the working people… public parks are imper-
atively needed and must be provided."[101] He argued that public parks were
every bit as necessary—unsentimentally necessary—as public education.

Self-interest. Finally, Cowan made a direct appeal to the wealthy: parks were an investment that would pay off, and a park system would create chic new neighborhoods for Louisville's wealthy citizens. He cited many cities—all Northern—to bolster his arguments. Chicago's parks had become profitable; New York had paid for Central Park through the revenues derived from wealthy adjacent properties.[102]

Not coincidentally, Cowan pointed specifically to the accomplishments of Frederick Law Olmsted: Central Park in New York, Prospect Park in Brooklyn, the Chicago parks (Washington and Jackson) near the neighborhood of Hyde Park, and, most pertinently, the park system of Buffalo. Buffalo was especially relevant for many reasons, but likely one of the most persuasive was financial. Buffalo's park commissioners claimed that their parks had raised local property values by as much as 300 percent, leading to higher property tax revenues, which had all but paid for the parks.

Of course, upper class, exclusive, segregated parks could just as easily—perhaps more easily—increase surrounding property values and give the wealthy a new cluster of desirable neighborhoods. So Cowan made another appeal for parks open to all—this time, couching it in terms of what we would now call talent attraction: the nicer Louisville was, the more likely skilled workers would stay. It was the kind of language that could make a factory-owner want to have a park system open to his employees. Again, he pointed to New York, where Central Park was "free to all the people, irrespective of condition or place."[103]

All this would have made a strong argument for parks in the abstract. But Cowan did more than explain why parks were necessary; he laid out a specific vision, clearly borrowed from Buffalo's Olmsted Park system: three large parks connected by a system of parkways. One park in the East End, perhaps up to 850 acres, with the Ohio River as its northern border and connected to a "grand boulevard" where large, expensive homes could line the road (of course, this boulevard would allow a long stretch of wealthy landowners to sell property at greatly increased values).[104] Then a park in the West End, on the city's western border with the river, where steep bluffs and the background of Indiana's hills would ensure that "a more beautiful park can hardly be described." Finally, a park in the South End, where current landowners had kept some land "in park-like condition."

Cowan, like Olmsted, wanted to build parks for the city's future, not its present. It was important, he said, to build them on a large scale in order to accommodate the city's population in fifty years—*fifty years!*—an era neither he, nor almost anyone else involved would live to see. "The parks will… influence thousands to make their homes here who would otherwise pass us by, will add to the wealth and stimulate the business of the city, and will surely repay their entire cost in many ways," he wrote.

On top of all of this was a sense of urgency. So many Northern cities now had parks that Louisville, which had industrialized like a Northern city, was noteworthy for not having them. That's what Cowan meant when he compared Louisville unfavorably to Cincinnati. Other Southern cities might not have parks, but they were poor; Louisville was not poor. Its barrenness amidst its riches was embarrassing. Besides, land was cheap now, and the cheaper the land, the more likely its increase in value could pay for the parks.

Cowan's essay effectively launched the first successful campaign for substantial public parks in the city's history, while Cowan himself remained almost entirely behind the scenes.

There were some concerns in the Salmagundi Club that promoting the parks plan would politicize the Club. So they decided to seek the support of the Commercial Club. Cowan, Speed, and the lawyer John Mason Brown went down to the Commercial Club to pitch the idea. Cowan did most of the talking (Speed demurred), and was again persuasive. One of the Commercial Club members, Morton Casseday, suggested using some wooded land along the Middle Fork for Beargrass Creek, which belonged to the Morton and Griswold estates for the Eastern Park. Cowan agreed to take a look at it, but he still expected the Eastern Park to be located near the city's waterworks along the Ohio River.[105]

The Commercial Club asked Brown to draft model legislation authorizing a park commission and bond referendum to enact Cowan's parks plan. Cowan passed along his extensive research to Brown—similar park acts and reports from cities across the country—and Brown drafted the proposed bill.[106]

A real movement for parks had begun.

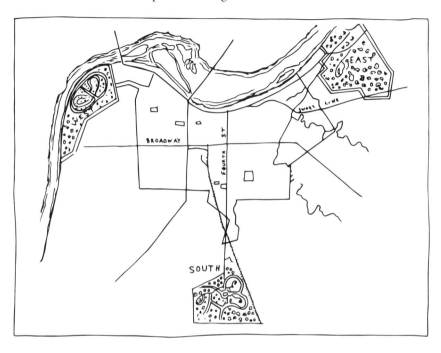

The original sketch of where Cowan's proposed parks might be sited. The Western and Southern parks are almost exactly where Shawnee and Iroquois parks are today. However, the Eastern Park ended up being built to the south of its proposed location here, along the Middle Fork of Beargrass Creek, instead of the banks of the Ohio River.[107]

CHAPTER 4

PARKS ARE POLITICAL

Charles Jacob was destined for a kind of glory and a kind of failure.

He was small but handsome, with dark, curly hair. He dressed like an aristocrat, which, in fact, he was—the son of one of the richest men in the city.[108] If Jacob's intellect and sophistication were not overwhelming, his self-confidence was. He also had some good qualities. A contemporary named Temple Bodley described Jacob as "absolutely incorruptible and fearless, generous, affectionate, a staunch friend."[109]

Well, perhaps not *completely* incorruptible. Pretty much everyone knew that he had bribed his way to the Louisville mayoralty over popular incumbent John Baxter in the 1872 Democratic primary (since Louisville was virtually a one-party town, winning the primary was tantamount to being elected). Jacob became the youngest mayor in the city's history at age 32.[110] He was re-elected in 1875* and served until 1879, when he had to take a legislatively mandated break. When he returned in 1881, he received an impressive—nigh dictatorial—95 percent of the vote.[111]

Like many proud men, Jacob's "singular susceptibility to flattery," wrote Bodley, made him "the dupe of designing and flattering satellites."[112] Over time, Jacob's sycophants manipulated him into pressing or crossing the limits

---

*   *Louisville's mayoral terms were then three years.*

of the law. Eventually, the backlash created by his autocratic tendencies allowed another political faction to rise, backed by the brothers Jim and John Whallen. (Once in power, they would prove no more law-abiding or less autocratic.)

The Whallens were smart enough not to seek office in their own right; as the owners of a burlesque theater, they knew how to run a show from behind the curtain. Booker Reed was their candidate. Like Jacob, Reed was from a wealthy, prominent family. But in many ways he was Jacob's opposite. Where Jacob was small and immaculate, Reed was "tall, shaggy, raw boned, loose jointed, strong-jawed like Pizarro." Reed dressed like a slob, consorted with rowdy company, had a quick and mighty temper, and swore like a soldier from beneath his Civil War beard. He was a bad enemy to have; yet, Reed possessed a self-awareness that Jacob lacked. He knew he had limitations. Perhaps he even knew he was not above being manipulated by powerful interests.

With the backing of Whallen brothers, Reed was elected mayor with 78 percent of the vote in 1884. He was still mayor when Cowan's Salmagundi paper was published in 1887, but he was a lame duck at the end of his term. Whether because of his vindictiveness or his principles, Reed had few friends left on the City Council. If fact, the Council favored the special interests and was already looking towards Reed's successor—who was also his predecessor— the past-and-future mayor, Charles Jacob.

Greed, personal animosity, and political conflict all ran rampant as governing broke down. The dysfunction that followed led to an episode called The Gas War.

The Louisville Gas Company had long enjoyed a local monopoly, but its privilege was up for renewal from the Louisville General Council and the Kentucky legislature. Mayor Reed was not entirely opposed to the renewal, but he wanted to make sure it came with stipulations that the gas plant and operations would be evaluated, that the Company was selling quality gas, and that the prices were fair. The Gas Company backed an alternative charter that would extend their monopoly for fifty years, with no quality control, and a high ceiling on the price they could charge.

Reed sent his proposal to the General Council; the Gas Company sent theirs. The Council ignored Reed and brought the Gas Company charter to committee. Not surprisingly, the Gas Company charter was unpopular. Also unsurprising, Reed announced he would veto it if passed by the full council. At a hearing of the special Gas Committee, Mayor Reed accused the Gas Company of bribing the Council. Then he lost his famous temper and got into a brawl with a Gas Company representative.[113]

This was the environment into which Cowan's park plan was launched. This was the political apparatus upon which it depended.

These twin threats—politics and greed—stalked Cowan's parks plan from the moment it debuted until far beyond when the shovels stopped digging. And at this early stage—when the park system was still just an idea, a report from a rich men's debating society and an article in the *Courier-Journal*—politics and greed were existential threats. The Gas War could have easily consigned Cowan's park plan to the long list of other failed attempts.[114] And so, finding himself and his plan in the midst of a political (and indeed physical) fracas, Cowan did something unusual: he stepped out and made a public case against the Gas Company.[115]

Cowan wrote an op-ed in the *Courier-Journal* and outlined everything wrong with the Gas Company's proposal. Perhaps to his surprise, the president of the company answered with an op-ed of his own. Cowan answered back. The president answered again. Cowan replied again.

This highly public exchange either helped or, more likely, coincided with a decisive public opinion shift against the gas bill. Cowan pressed his advantage and addressed the Board of Trade, despite worries that his heretical Republicanism would be a hindrance. He needn't have worried. The Gas bill died. Cowan won. It was a testament to his tact, his friendships, and his political skills that this Yankee Republican was able to successfully orchestrate such a high-level political coup against powerful moneyed interests.[116] But it wasn't without cost: Cowan had exhausted himself. More importantly, Cowan winning meant Jacob had lost. And in November, Jacob won his third term, despite not being the nominee of either major party. The new mayor, same as the old mayor, could be a fatal enemy to the parks plan.

John Mason Brown, at least, had maintained friendly relations with both

Cowan and Jacob. He had avoided getting involved in the Gas War. Now, Brown had the delicate task of winning Jacob over to the parks bill, despite Cowan's involvement.

Jacob dragged his feet. Two weeks before the legislature adjourned, he relented and offered tepid support.

Brown went to Cowan's office. "Here Cowan, I have, at last, got Mayor Jacob's approval," he said. "Now take this Act to Frankfort and pass it."[117]

"It is impossible Colonel," Cowan told him. "My health has broken down under the great strain I have undergone in the fight against the Gas Company Charter; besides, I do not believe that any man could get a new bill through so late in this legislative session."

"Well, you know that all sorts of mischief may be done before the next Legislature meets," Brown replied as he turned and walked away. [118]

How right he was. In those days, the legislature only met once every two years.[119] It would be 1890 before the parks bill could be taken up again.[120] And Jacob's opposition was only one of the possible threats to Cowan's park plan. The wrong kind of support could be just as detrimental.

CHAPTER 5

THE SOUTHERN PARK

In 1888, just six miles south of the Louisville city limits lay the kind of hill they called a knob—so steep that some of them could never be farmed, pockets of woods that may never have been logged, trees so large they were considered ancient even in the 1880s.[121] At the very top was a 20-acre prairie-pasture, so that the whole hill was tonsured like a monk's head.

Before the European conquest, American Indians set fire to vast swaths of prairie and woodland just like this. In the Rocky Mountains, they entertained Meriwether Lewis and William Clark by torching sappy fir trees into spectacular flame.[122] In New York, one colonist wrote "such a fire is a splendid sight when one sails on the rivers at night while the forest is ablaze on both banks."[123]

But far from destroying the woods, these regular burnings kept them thinned out, giving the great trees so much space to grow that white settlers in Ohio had thought the wild woods looked like English parks.[124] These spacious woods allowed for abundant game, nuts, and blackberry brambles. A horse could ride at a gallop between the trees.[125]

The knob in Louisville must have been one of these torched places, for the Europeans named it "Burnt Knob." Perhaps this ancient Indian forestry was why the woods of Burnt Knob were so beautiful. It was a lovely hill with great lovely woods sloping down all sides. Tall trees checkered the sunlight making its way down to a mat of darkening leaves.

It was easy to see how Burnt Knob could be made into a park.

A group of landowners invited the newly reelected Mayor Jacob to see Burnt Knob. One of the men was Meriwether Lewis Clark, founder of the Kentucky Derby, builder and manager of the nearby (and struggling) Churchill Downs, and grandson of the great explorer William Clark.[126]

They showed Jacob the hill, the view, fed him a fine lunch in a cabin at the summit. This was the park for him, the park for Louisville, they told him. Just like the Salmagundi Club said! Parks for the people!

Jacob agreed. He promised to buy it on the spot with his own money. Surely the city would pay him back.[127]

Even before Jacob was reelected, there had been schemes to sell supposedly park-ready land to the city at inflated prices. Cowan's park proposal was chum in the water for local land sharks.[128]

In one such scheme, three men named Moore, Bremaker, and Dulaney bought a 600-acre tract for about $132,000 (roughly $3.3 million in today's dollars).[129] They conveyed it to the Southern Heights Land Company, comprised of three men named Moore, Bremaker, and Dulaney.[130] The Company then aimed to sell the tract, including an area called Highland Park, to the city for $400,000 (something like $10,000,000 today).[131] With a hop, skip, and a jump, they would almost triple their money.

An ordinance was introduced to the General Council to authorize the purchase of the Southern Heights land and to make it the city's sole park. A park project of that size would essentially doom any chance of Cowan's multi-park system.[132] Cowan caught wind of the plan, and suspecting that a majority of the council had already secretly agreed to the scheme,[133] wrote a pseudonymous letter to the *Courier-Journal* attacking it as an idea as cooked up by politicians. "Go slow, gentlemen," he cautioned the Council, saying they should "under no circumstances" pay more that $120,000 for the property. If the ordinance were put to a referendum, Cowan asserted, it would be "overwhelmingly defeated unless boodle is freely used to buy voters and influence."[134] The "proper course," he countered, would be to have the state legislature authorize a park commission, as had been done in other cities, and then put the plan to a public referendum.[135]

Cowan's letter, along with the opposition of a watchdog group called the Association of Louisville, were evidently enough to kill the Highland Park plan. At a contentious meeting of the Commercial Club, one of the Southern Heights landowners announced that the Highland Park ordinance would be withdrawn.[136]

Since Mayor Jacob had bought Burnt Knob with his own money, he hadn't worried about whether a state law or city ordinance authorized the purchase. Jacob persuaded the city council to buy the land from him for exactly what he paid, plus interest.[137] It must have been the largest petty cash purchase in Louisville history.

But, it turned out that Jacob had not actually bought Burnt Knob. He had bought only the north side of Burnt Knob, a side lacking those ancient and most beautiful woods, lacking sufficient space to cut a road to the top of the hill, lacking the entire plateau at the top of the knob, lacking really quite a lot.[138]

According to the city charter, the General Council could not establish a park without a public referendum. And, since Cowan's park bill had not yet passed, the state legislature had not created a park commission nor authorized it to hold such a referendum.

Jacob and the Council ignored the charter. The Council passed an ordinance to buy the land from Jacob for a public park.

They named it "Jacob Park."[139]

Jacob hired Meriwether Lewis Clark, happy seller of the land, as Chief of Parks at a salary of $3,000 a year (about $75,000 today) and a Park Superintendent named Manlius Taylor (grand-nephew of the ignominious antebellum president Zachary Taylor) at half that pay. [140]

Clark and Taylor set about "improving" the park, as they understood it. According to the *Courier-Journal*, Taylor "wonderfully" changed "the wilderness of woods and hills and valleys" that had been Burnt Knob. [141] But according to Temple Bodley, a Taylor was "a well meaning but wholly incompetent countryman" who butchered the woods, tragically and permanently, with both fire and axe. [142]

Additionally, Jacob hired a civil engineer with no knowledge of landscape architecture to cut a road from the base of the hill to its summit. The grading was excessively steep, and in winding up the hill, the road, at several points, crossed the property of William Stewart, for which the city had neither title nor permission. [143] Andrew Cowan thought the roads at the top of the hill looked "like a coon's track." [144]

When Henry Codman, Frederick Law Olmsted's trusted lieutenant, finally visited the park a year later, he marveled at these roads. "An entirely incompetent man… has graded some of the most wonderful roads I have ever seen," Codman reported to Olmsted. "He seemed to think nothing of twenty and thirty foot cuts and fills, and of course these have absolutely straight and very steep slopes." [145] It was enough to make Codman despair. "The money which has been expended upon the land"—some $100,000—"has been most outrageously used, and the results and present condition of affairs are anything but hopeful there." [146]

At the same time, Jacob had directed the construction of a "Grand Boulevard," which was to connect the park to Third Avenue, and in doing so pass right by Meriwether Lewis Clark's racing track, Churchill Downs. [147] No doubt, any increased traffic to Clark's racetrack was incidental to his involvement in the park and boulevard enterprises.

Now that there was a city park, the land rush was on. "Land companies sprang up like mushrooms, to get the benefit of an expected boom in the neighborhood of the Park," and along the road, Cowan remembered. [148] The only land title Jacob had bothered to obtain along Grand Boulevard was owned by one of these companies.[149] The other landowners, whose property had pretty clearly been seized without due process, sued the city.

Clark and Taylor undertook to put in other roads, to connect to Grand Boulevard. They named one of them "Taylor Boulevard."[150]

The city dedicated Jacob Park on June 1, 1889.[151]

As for Mayor Jacob, the strain of the whole thing had been too much. He was consumed with anxiety about the money he had "outrageously"—and illegally—spent on Burnt Knob and its Grand Boulevard.

Perhaps in his previous terms, he could have handled these baying hounds of probity, made them heel, run for re-election on an Independent ticket and still beat anyone who dared snipe at the personal sacrifices he'd made for his city. Perhaps once, but no longer.

Mayor Jacob quit. He fled to Europe to recover his health, leaving William Lyons as acting mayor for four months. He would never be mayor again.[152]

But before he ran away, Jacob swung one more hatchet into Cowan's vision for parks.[153]

Chapter 6

The Beargrass Valley

Andrew Cowan hiked up the Beargrass valley of the Morton and Griswold estates that Morton Casseday had recommended at the Commercial Club three years earlier, as well as the adjoining McFerran woods. It had snowed in December, turning these woods into a world of black and white: white snow, dark trees, the creek darkest of all, a ribbon wending through the hills.[154] Chickadees, also black and white, with a seesawing song, *see-bee see-bay*.

Cowan hiked through the snow-dusted trunks, the ragweed reeds exploding with ice. He came to the beginning of a one-sided limestone canyon. It started small, undulated, and grew until the walls reached over thirty feet high. Beargrass Creek had been working on that wall for eons, and for eons the limestone had resisted. And yet, if Cowan touched it now, he could break off a fossil 400 million years old with little thought. Once, a great flat boulder had broken off and landed in the creek and dammed up a little pool where fish could swim in place. Folks called it Big Rock.

Along one bank was a sycamore with three trunks. People called it "The Three Sisters." In later years, they would try to shore up two of the rotting trunks with a fill of concrete and rebar. It was a futile effort. In the end, there would be only one sister and two concrete ghosts.

Cowan hiked up the Beargrass valley, from the McFerran woods to the Breckinridge farm east of Big Rock. Altogether, there must have been four hundred acres of woodland, pasture, and creek. He thought it was perfect. Here was land that could make a park equal to any in the country.[155]

Cowan got to work. He consulted a friend of his, Judge John Barr, about the land. The good judge quickly secured options for the Morton and Griswold land. He then committed several breaches of professional ethics and told Cowan that Mrs. Hattie Bonnycastle owned some additional land on the southeast side of the Morton and Griswold woods. Barr knew the land was heavily mortgaged, that Mrs. Bonnycastle was having trouble paying the interest. She might well be willing to sell. Judge Barr secured an option from her for sixty acres.

Cowan additionally secured options from Mrs. Alexander and Mrs. Cochran and then Mrs. Barret, who owned some hilly land on the east side of Bonnycastle's, along the southwest side of the creek.[156]

When Cowan got back to his house on Fourth Avenue, he sat in the library. It dawned on him that all of the options were given by widows and executors—people who would soon have sold the land one way or another, likely for real estate developments, which would have made it too expensive for a public park. He had gotten to them just in time. Cowan couldn't believe the city's good fortune.[157]

But if the Eastern Park was to have a brighter fate than the hijacked Southern Park, Cowan needed to get the Park Act passed by the state legislature.

And it was at this moment that, his partner in that effort—John Mason Brown—suddenly died.

CHAPTER 7

THE BOARD OF PARK COMMISSIONERS

John Mason Brown died before the legislature could convene again. His law partner, George Davie, took over the job of shepherding the park bill through the legislature.

An increasingly anxious Mayor Jacob had demanded, as a condition of his assent, that Davie amend the park bill to include a provision requiring any park board to accept Burnt Knob as it was and to pay back the $100,000 (about $2.6 million today) that Jacob had spent hacking the park in the name of improving it. Even worse, Jacob demanded that Davie to pare Cowan's three proposed parks down to one.[158]

Despite winning Jacob's approval at such a steep price, Davie was still stymied in the legislature. Cowan suspected that Booker Reed was holding up the bill to spite to his old rival.

"Cowan," he said, "we want you to go to Frankfort [the state capital] with us tomorrow morning… . The Park Act is in danger," Davie told him.[159]

But Cowan was bedridden with a "bilious attack." "Davie, I am almost too sick to walk across this room," he said. "I can't go. What could I do anyway?"

"We believe that [state legislator] Arthur Wallace is holding up the Park Act to oblige his friend Booker Reed, who has it in for Jacob. You are a friend of Arthur Wallace and he likes you. You must go with us tomorrow morning."

So Cowan went. He met with Wallace and explained the park bill. Wallace relented.[160]

And so, after three years of hard effort, the Park Act finally passed on May 6, 1890. It set up a quick special election for the Board of Park Commissioners on July 1st, followed by a referendum on the Park Act itself a month later.[161]

Davie wanted Cowan to run for one of the six seats on the Park Commission. Cowan resisted; he claimed his business was too consuming and that he'd already done what he could for the parks.

What's more likely is that Cowan, the Republican carpetbagger, doubted his ability to win an election in heavily Democratic Louisville (Democrats being, in those days, associated with the South and Confederate sympathies). If that was the case, his fears were soon justified.[162]

Cowan and Brown had tried to design the Park Act in such a way to prevent the Park Commission from becoming a partisan cash dispensary. But it looked like that might happen anyway. Davie told Cowan that John Breckinridge Castleman was trying to run six commissioners on an exclusively Democratic ticket, and he would not let Cowan join it.[163]

Cowan was incredulous: Castleman? John Breckinridge Castleman? Since when did he care about the parks?[164]

John Breckinridge Castleman was a Southern aristocrat of the plantation variety—the kind who grew up on an estate named after his family ("Castleton"), in a mansion paneled with marble and mahogany and crimson satin on the rosewood furniture.[165] The kind who had a black "mammy" whom he called "Aunt Hanna" and a bevy of other slaves with insidiously familial names—Uncle John, Uncle Anthony, Aunt Beckie, Aunt Susana. And literally an Uncle Ben and Aunt Jemima. Slaves for milking, slaves for cooking, slaves for keeping the house.[166] Castleman had been especially fond of Uncle Isaac the head butler, whose funeral he would attend many years later, and whom the *Courier-Journal* would eulogize fondly as "a typical old-fashioned darky."[167] Then there was Uncle Simon, the inimitable banjo-picking slave, whom Castleman remembered for entertaining his father's guests with songs he would remember his entire life, though he was just eleven years old when Simon died and just twelve when his father followed suit.[168]

Castleman also remembered the colors of the roses and other exotic flowers his widowed mother kept in the greenhouse and the garden, how she cultivated nature.[169]

John Breckinridge Castleman

When the Civil War broke out, Castleman became one of Morgan's Raiders, cavalrymen who foraged and sabotaged deep into Northern-controlled territory. For a time, they wreaked havoc on a much larger Union Army, but in the end they were defeated, and Castleman could no longer be a Morgan's Raider. So he became a Confederate spy. [170, 171]

There were secret, Confederate-sympathizing societies in the Midwest. One of them was called the Sons of Liberty, and some of the Sons of Liberty wanted the Midwest to secede from the Union and join the Confederacy, dealing the North a body blow just as the war seemed to be grinding toward an inevitable Union victory. Castleman and his small cohort planned to use these groups to spark a revolt in the North against the Union government.[172]

But there was a flaw in this plan: many of these groups had been infiltrated by Union spies. In fact, Castleman thought, in retrospect, that there had been men with him the whole time who were untrustworthy, unreliable.[173] And he was right. The Northern revolt never happened. The conspiracy was busted; Castleman was captured.

He became a prisoner of war at Camp Morton, near Indianapolis. People died all the time in Civil War prison camps, and not just from capital punishment. Word of the notorious Confederate camp in Andersonville, Georgia had gotten out. Tales of its skeletal prisoners, rotting to death from scurvy and dysentery, had reached the North, and the North had taken offense. Some Northerners now considered it their patriotic duty to mistreat Confederate POWs in retaliation.[174]

In solitary confinement, in a 7' x 7' cell, Castleman complained that his treatment had been very hard indeed. [175, 176]

At least he was allowed a pipe, which quickly developed into a nervous habit. He smoked ten hours a day, "thereby injuring my health," as he would later remember.[177] In his tiny cell, as he smoked and smoked and smoked, Castleman thought of revenge that would never come and a country that would never come about and the likelihood that the end of his life would probably come soon.[178]

There was a way out, perhaps, if he could countenance it. Indeed, it was an out many of his compatriots were taking—a Union loyalty oath in exchange for their freedom. But if that was how little those "damned scoundrels" thought of the Confederate project, thought Castleman, then so be it. They didn't deserve a country anyway.[179]

After so many betrayals, it was hard to trust anyone. Just recently a man had ratted out some fellow prisoners in order to save himself. If that ever happened to Castleman, God help the rat—he'd wish he'd never been born.[180]

Castleman's mother smuggled him a Bible with passages underlined by his spymaster, Thomas Henry Hines, who was still at large:

"Let not your heart be troubled… "

"And if I go and prepare a place for you, I come again…"

"And whither I go, ye know the way."

"And whatsoever ye shall ask in My name, that will I do…"

"I will not leave you comfortless, I will come to you."

And Castleman did take comfort.[181] If he thought of death, he didn't say anything about it in his letters—didn't mention it, though followed him like a shadow in the valley of Camp Morton.

His chances looked grim. Espionage is a capital offense at any time, let alone during a civil war. Only President Lincoln himself could definitively save the young Confederate Major.

Incredibly, that is almost what happened.[182]

On November 30, 1864, Castleman's Unionist brother-in-law, Judge Samuel Miller Breckinridge, visited President Lincoln at the White House.[183] It was just three weeks after Lincoln's re-election and almost four years into his the Civil War. The president's face, famously, had become a specter. He was evidently relieved to have the diversion of Sam Breckinridge, the judge from Kentucky. Lincoln had also been born in Kentucky, and so they talked about Kentuckians they knew in common. They talked for almost two hours, until the President looked at the clock and said, "Well, well, Sam, I have so much enjoyed having you with me that I have been glad for the time to forget grave questions that beset the country, but we have neglected the interest that brings you here," which was clemency for the prisoner John Breckenridge Castleman.[184] Lincoln mentioned that he had a cabinet meeting in fifteen minutes. "I will give you now in the strictest confidence a note only to be used in case of emergency. Meantime, from what I learn, it would be best to have that boy's attorneys endeavor to postpone the trial, for those young Confederates have caused the government annoyances and expense."[185]

Lincoln's note read:[186]

Major General Hovey, or
Whomsoever may have charge.
Whenever John B. Castleman shall be tried,
if convicted and sentenced, suspend execution until
further order from me, and send me the record.

A. Lincoln

Five months later, the war was over, and the top generals for each side, Ulysses S Grant and Robert E. Lee, negotiated a prisoner exchange, which was to include Castleman. And then, just five days later, President Lincoln was assassinated by a pro-Confederate cabal (whose members also nearly killed Secretary of State William Seward, badly wounding both him and his son, Fred, and planned on killing Vice President Andrew Johnson before that particular would-be assassin changed his mind).[187] Castleman had lost his emergency get-out-of-jail free card.[188]

As it happened, Castleman's cohort of prisoners had been transferred to Washington, DC., arriving just four days after Lincoln's murder.[189] With Washington in turmoil, Castleman was thrown into a cell at the Old Capital Prison with twenty other people, including a fellow Kentuckian, Colonel Albert Berry, who would later serve in Congress. Perhaps the Old Capital Prison was an improvement over Camp Morton, or perhaps Castleman was simply made of stern stuff, but he never complained to his fellow prisoners, not of the quarters, not of the food, not of the fact that he was still a prisoner.[190]

At the stroke of midnight on his second night there, a guard entered the prison cell. "Castleman," he called out. As Castleman walked to the door, Colonel Berry grabbed his hand, thinking his new friend would soon be shot.[191] But, he needn't have worried, yet.

Castleman was transferred back to Indianapolis to stand trial.[192] The result of the trial was conviction on six charges of espionage, inciting insurrection, destruction of government property, and violating the laws of war. But rather than execution, his sentence was exile.[193]

It only lasted a year. His influential friends and family successfully appealed to President Andrew Johnson, himself a Southerner, for a full pardon.[194]

By 1867, Castleman was back in Kentucky. Like Cowan, he settled in Louisville.[195] Eventually, he bought some land east of town called Schwartz Woods. He named it Castlewood and set about trying to sell it or raise its value by any means by possible.

Castleman and Cowan were in many ways similar and in many ways opposites. Both were post-war transplants to Louisville. Both were successful businessmen. Both were respected civic leaders, both were members of the Salmagundi Club.

But the opposites were what stood out. Castleman was an aristocrat, Cowan a self-made success. Castleman was a Dixie Democrat; Cowan was a Yankee Republican. Castleman was a peacock; Cowan kept a low profile.

And there was something else, something about Colonel Castleman that Colonel Cowan didn't like, didn't trust, just didn't quite believe. "I had never before heard Castleman's name mentioned in connection with Parks," he later wrote. "I am sure that until then Colonel Castleman had not been 'conspicuous' in anything relating to Public Parks for Louisville."[196]

So why on earth was *Castleman* running a slate of Park Commissioners?

Well, it just so happened John Breckinridge Castleman knew of some land east of town that he thought would be just perfect for a park—his land. He thought he would like to sell it to the Board of Park Commissioners. To do so, it seemed that it would help to be *on* the Board of Park Commissioners. And to have friends on the Board of Park Commissioners.

Besides that, if Castleman pushed through a solidly Democratic Park Commission, money would be easy to dispense to whomever they wanted.

A few days after Castleman announced the Democratic slate, a group of businessmen, including Major Ed McDonald of the Kentucky Title Company, organized an opposition ticket. They wanted Cowan to lead the ticket. "Colonel Cowan, if those Democrats are elected," McDonald said, "we know that the bulk of the Park Bonds will be spent on Jacob's Park and Boulevard, for the benefit of the Southern Heights Land Company."[197] Cowan agreed. And so he ran, heading up what would be dubbed "the Calico Ticket" because of its partisan diversity.

It seemed pre-ordained that the Democrats would win. Until they didn't. On election day, only two members of Castleman's ticket were elected—Gottlieb Layer and Castleman himself—the other four were Calicos: Democrats Thomas Sherley and John Finzer, and Republicans Andrew Cowan and E.C. Bohne.[198]

Cowan later realized that the Calico Ticket had succeeded largely because of help from John Finzer's son-in-law, Billy Bailey, who had created a political organization to elect himself jailer and then used the same organization to help elect Finzer. Cowan and Bohne had won almost incidentally, despite their Republican affiliation, and with the least number of votes of any of the winners.

Next was the referendum on the Park Act itself. Cowan feared that the Democratic machine, having failed to win the Park Commission, would work to spike the Park Act. The public was generally apathetic to the second of two special elections in the middle of the summer. A small number of votes could have swung it either way. Again, Bailey's organization came to the rescue and canvassed support for the Park Act. At 10:00 on election night, Castleman walked into the office of acting mayor William Lyons. "The Park Act is defeated," Castleman announced.[199] Cowan was in the mayor's office, too, hidden by a desk. At Castleman's proclamation, Cowan stood up and said, "You are mistaken, Colonel. I am satisfied the Park Act is safe—but it is by a small vote and narrow margin."[200]

Cowan was right. Bailey's machine had carried the day once more. "I am glad to hear it," Castleman replied, no doubt turning on his heels and leaving in a huff.[201]

Soon, Cowan and Castleman were back in the mayor's office as members of the new Board of Park Commissioners, which met in full and drew lots to decide how the terms would be staggered—two would serve for a year before facing election, two for two years, and two for three. Ironically, the two Republicans—Cowan and Bohne—drew the three and two-year terms, respectively. "Fortunately for the public," Cowan would later write, "for we could not have been elected again."[202]

The next order of business was for the Board to elect a president. Apparently, Castleman's friends encouraged Cowan to vote for Castleman. Cowan would do no such thing.

It took the small Board seventeen ballots to elect a president, but in the end it was Thomas Sherley, not Castleman, who won.

In March 1891, the park bonds were finally sold. After years of Cowan's effort, Louisville finally had the legislative authority, the legal process, and the money to build the parks.

However, politics and greed had not finished threatening Cowan's park plan.[203] Castleman, for one, was still on the Park Commission and still owned those twenty acres of wooded land east of town. Already, he was lobbying his Board colleagues to buy the land and make it the Eastern Park.

Cowan had other ideas.[204] Olmsted was the answer. Olmsted could make the difference. If Cowan could just get his attention.

CHAPTER 8

FREDERICK LAW OLMSTED WAS A GENIUS

Chicago 1893.

It was a plaster utopia in perfect white—arches, columns, colonnades, statues—a beautiful, magical, fake world that had taken some of the best architectural and landscape minds, and thousands of artists and workers, two years to put together.[205]

Louisville sculptor Enid Yandell was one of those artists. Just 24 years old, with dark eyebrows and dark, sad eyes, a pretty chin and a serious mouth, dark hair under a beret, She had worked 16-hour days to get to *this* place, *this* moment.[206]

Leaning her athletic, Victorian-clad frame onto her most-anticipated sculpture—a 7-foot Daniel Boone for the Kentucky Building—Yandell looked at the camera from under those dark eyebrows.[207] "Sculpture builds muscles," she said. "It is better than sports for muscle building."[208]

But, "my hands and arms get so tired," she confessed.[209] She'd been sculpting clay copies of Greek marble masterpieces for the Woman's Building, working her hands through a ton of clay a day for $5—equivalent to about $129 a day now.[210] Not bad wages, but not great considering the hours she worked.[211]

If she ever got a chance to breathe, she might have sensed that all her work, all the exhausting work, might be worth it.[212] There would be *thousands* of tourists walking here, *tens* of thousands, *hundreds* of thousands, swarms of people on these same aromatic allés. They would come and they would see Daniel Boone in a raccoon-skin hat and deerskin jacket with leather fringe, jaw grimly set, powder horn rubbing against his hip, eyes squinting at the vanishing American Frontier, hands ready and relaxed on a long rifle.[213] The very image of resolute masculinity sculpted, in plaster, by young Enid Yandell of Louisville, Kentucky.

Yandell had been selected for this pageant by a group of her late father's friends (including Andrew Cowan) who had commissioned her—paying her roughly $39,000 in today's dollars to sculpt something to represent the state at the Kentucky Building of the Exposition.[214]

Yandell's Boone sculpture won one of three medals given to women at the Exposition. In a year, she would apprentice for Auguste Rodin in Paris. She was on her way.

If the World's Colombian Exposition was the beginning of Enid Yandell's career, it was but one ray of light in the brilliant sunset of Frederick Law Olmsted's career.

Olmsted was like a Mozart of the landscape, each plant, each hill, each line a note in a living symphony. He could look at a topographical map or a representation of a tree and put himself *there*. On the ground. He could imagine what it would actually *feel* like. He knew the ambient impact of a beech versus a maple versus an oak. He understood how the light would play on the leaves and which leaves and which light. He could use plants as perfume to create the right smell for the occasion.[215]

The Exposition was one of the most ambitious temporary undertakings of any American city, ever. Chicago, the host city, wanted to outdo Paris's already famous 1889 Exposition, which had awed attendees and bequeathed the city with the Eiffel Tower.[216]

Daniel Burnham led the enterprise. A famous architect in his own right—he and his business partner John Root had pioneered the skyscraper—Burnham sought other renowned architects to design the Exposition's temporary buildings on a scale of grandeur reminiscent of a Renaissance city-state.[217]

But first he sought Olmsted.[218] For more than three decades, Olmsted had been the dominant landscape architect in the United States. If Burnham wanted the best, and he did, there would have been no second choices for landscape architect.[219] Olmsted was simply in a tier of his own. He was the most famous, strong-willed, and brilliant landscape architect in the country. He had literally invented the term "landscape architecture."[220]

At first, Olmsted turned down the Burnham's offer. He preferred to think in forty-year horizons; the Exposition would be done and gone in little more than three.[221] He also held a dim view of Chicago's architectural ambition, in which Burnham had been instrumental. He thought Chicago "had a weakness for 'big things,' and liked to think that it was outbuilding New York… The faults of construction as well as of art in its great showy buildings must have been numerous. Their walls were thin, and were often overweighted with gross and coarse misornamentation."[222]

On the other hand, Exposition might be just the opportunity Olmsted needed to finally raise the profile of landscape architecture, to give it public credibility and respect equal to architecture or any other fine art.

Olmsted changed his mind. After all, he was ambitious, too. He accepted Burnham's offer for a fee equivalent to about $560,000 today.[223]

Olmsted found in Burnham an employer who was resolute, visionary, blunt, inspiring. Burnham worked so many hours on the Exposition that he lived in an on-site trailer. Above his desk was the word RUSH.[224] He was a man who perfectly channeled Chicago's ambitions. Olmsted liked him.[225]

Olmsted brought along his pudgy 29-year-old wunderkind Harry Codman. Codman had the energy of his years and landscape wisdom way beyond them. At age 25, he had studied under Edouard François André—the Frederick Law Olmsted of France—and then apprenticed for Olmsted back in Brookline. At 27 he had joined Olmsted's firm and quickly become a full partner.[226]

After Olmsted's son John, Codman was the person Olmsted leaned on the most to get through his tremendous workload (in addition to the Exposition, the firm was juggling projects in Boston, Rochester (New York), and at the grounds of the Biltmore Estate, which Olmsted saw as one of his most important legacies).[227]

When Olmsted looked at Lake Michigan, his eyes were the color of the Lake. And when he looked at the Lake with his Lake-blue, grey-blue eyes, he saw as broad an expanse as those eyes could take in. In those eyes, the Lake was Chicago's only beauty.[228] And as he looked at the endless water of the Lake, Olmsted envisioned more water—a series of lagoons, water next to the water. And on these lagoons, Olmsted saw boats, silent electric boats gliding on the water next to the water, little quiet launches gracefully cutting the still water into a thousand flashes of the sun. That's what Olmsted wanted. Silent boats gliding with "poetic mystery."[229] This could be a magical background for perhaps the greatest World's Fair ever held, if only he could get others to see it, too.

Olmsted narrowed in on Jackson Park, which ran along the lakeshore on the south side of Chicago. Even Codman couldn't quite see the appeal of Jackson Park; what he saw was six hundred acres of barren swamp.[230] Never mind. Olmsted marched forward, undeterred. They could dredge the marsh, dig the lagoons, build at a higher elevation on the excavated sand, and leave, in the middle of the largest lagoon, a wooded island—an artificial wilderness surrounded by civilization, a perfect microcosm of what Frederick Law Olmsted did best.

Burnham, and after some persuasion the Exposition board, agreed. Olmsted had carried the first and most important point; not all his victories would be so complete.[231] As his son John later wrote, "It was one of the greatest advantages that Father had that his employers usually grew to have such faith in him that they often were prepared to accept his recommendations without attempting to understand them."[232]

Really, it was hard to say how many people *did* understand Olmsted's work. He could draw, but he was not a draftsman.[233] Nor was he an architect, either by training or inclination. Nor was he a horticulturalist—in fact, he would later tell his youngest, Frederick Law, Jr., who went by "Rick," that he regretted his lack of botanical and arboricultural knowledge more than anything in his career.[234]

Not everyone recognized Olmsted's work as something that required planning. People thought his parks just *happened*. Where Olmsted's artistry had created meadows, people saw open space, *vacant* space "in which anything of public interest could be dumped."[235] "Suppose that you had been commissioned to build a really grand opera house," he wrote to his architect friend Henry Van Brunt, "[and] that after the construction work had been nearly completed and your scheme of decoration fully designed, you should be instructed that the building was to be used on Sundays as a Baptist Tabernacle, and that a suitable place must be made for a huge organ, a pulpit and a dipping pool."[236] He asked for Van Brunt's pardon of his outburst, explaining, "It is a matter of chronic anger with me."[237]

Furthermore, the Olmsted firm was not a one-man enterprise. He had partners, he had assistants, he had draftsmen and interns. In many ways, he was like a modern celebrity chef-restaurateur—he created the menu, he hired the staff, he scouted the locations, and he served as the public face of the organization. But he did not draw every line, every tree, or every park himself.

In fact, Olmsted was relying on others more and more. He was an old man now, older even than his 71 years. He had a white beard, leaned on a cane—his leg having once been crushed in a carriage accident[238]—his eyes, which could twinkle with intelligence or burn with indignation, often had the flat, dull look of someone exhausted, in constant poor health, mentally and physically.[239] Olmsted suffered from neuralgia (a condition usually associated with intense pain along the nerves in the head or face),[240] toothaches, and a constant roaring in his ears that was probably tinnitus—the same vexing condition that deafened Beethoven.[241] And several times throughout his life, especially after periods of prolonged work and stress, his depression was so bad he could so bad he could not read, write, sleep, or work for weeks or even months at a time.[242]

And yet, the firm's workload was greater than ever. The Chicago work alone would have been enough to bury a man half his age with twice his health.

Then, along came Harry Codman. Artistically, Codman was the son he never had.[243] Olmsted quickly began to trust his young partner's instincts.

Then he began to rely on him, to the extent that the World's Fair became a Harry Codman project supervised by Olmsted. Professionally, Olmsted trusted Codman more than he trusted anyone else. There was no other way he could have taken on both the Exposition and Biltmore at the same time.

Of course, Olmsted did have surviving sons. John and Frederick, Jr.— called "Rick"—were both half-brothers and first cousins (Olmsted having married his brother's widow), but they were 18 years apart.[244] Rick was too young to meaningfully contribute to the practice, though he would soon intern with Burnham in Chicago and Gifford Pinchot at Biltmore.[245] As for John, Olmsted doubted his visionary capacity. "You are not a man of genius of art," he had once written to a 22-year-old John. "A man of less artistic impulse I never knew."[246]

Perhaps this judgment was too severe, but John absorbed his father's anger, pushed back where he felt misjudged, resolved to do better where he thought Olmsted was right.[247]

But if Codman had the artistic half of Olmsted's abilities, John had the administrative half. John settled into the crucial role of running the firm from Brookline. When people wrote to the firm, it was more often than not John who was reading the letters, deciding what course of action was required, and writing the replies or communicating to Olmsted and Codman what was needed.[248]

In the main, Olmsted's vision for the Exposition was borne out. There were the lagoons, the wooded island—albeit with the addition of a Japanese temple—and a formal, rectangular basin surrounded by stunning classical architecture, which soon came to be known as The Court of Honor.

And all of it lay on the edge of the endless blue of the Lake.[249]

The Court of Honor, in particular, produced the kind of magical effects Olmsted intended.[250] (Though one observer had it that "one of the most magnificent spectacles of the World's Fair was presented by John B Castleman… riding a trio of five-gaited saddle horses exemplifying the perfection of the American saddle horse." Castleman seemed to agree.)[251]

It was a triumph of scenery. Burnham wanted everyone who entered the fair to come through the Court. He loved to take guests on special sunset tours of the Court lagoon, riding in electric boats cutting lines through the fading light.[252] Poetic mystery indeed. How grateful Burnham must have been, in those quiet moments of evening, for his famous landscape architect.

In March 1893, an architect named Charles McKim, his partner, Stanford White, and painter and sculptor Frank Millet threw a banquet at the original, ornate Madison Square Garden to celebrate the achievement—still underway—of the World's Colombian Exposition.[253] Burnham was there, of course, as were other prominent architects, painters, sculptors, writers, and art patrons. But neither McKim nor White nor Millet had seen fit to include landscape architecture in the program, as they had included architecture, painting, and sculpture.[254] Nor had they seen fit to hang celebratory banners for landscape architecture, as they did for the other three arts.[255]

If Olmsted's primary reason for joining the Exposition was to raise the profile of landscape architecture, to make it an equal of any other art of profession, it would seem he had failed.

When it came time for Burnham's speech, he tried to remedy the slight, saying of Olmsted: "Each of you knows the name and genius of him who stands first in the heart and confidence of American artists, the creator of your own and many other city parks…. An artist, he paints with lakes and wooded slopes; with lawns and banks and forest-covered hills; with mountainsides and ocean views. He should stand where I do tonight… "[256]

Coming from Burnham, a man of no modest ego, that was some praise.

"He it is who has been our best adviser and our common mentor. In the highest sense he is the planner of the Exposition—Fredrick Law Olmsted."

The crowd roared with applause.[257]

But Olmsted wasn't even there. He skipped the banquet; he never heard the applause that rang in Burnham's ears. And a century later, Olmsted was still more famous than all the men there.

Then it was over. "At last the Exposition is a thing of the past!" an exhausted member of the Exposition's Spanish delegation wrote to a friend. "Of course I am awfully glad of it, but this does not prevent me of having a feeling of sadness as when I see these beautiful grounds, and buildings yesterday crowded and today absolutely deserted!"[258] And they were—absolutely deserted.

In the end, the Exposition would be remembered, it would be missed, but it would not live, it would not last. The Exposition would not be Olmsted's legacy.

Nine months later it all burned to the ground.[259]

To the contrary, the Louisville parks would be one of the, lasting, masterpieces of a fading genius.

Chapter 9

Olmsted Comes to Louisville

In his office at 421 West Main Street—a five-story building with arched windows[260]—Andrew Cowan wrote a letter to the Olmsted firm, which was then in the midst of the busiest part of the Exposition work.

Without quite offering Olmsted the Louisville job—which, of course, he couldn't do, being just one of six park commissioners—Cowan informed Olmsted of Louisville's need for a landscape architect and asked for his advice on the best course of action and how soon he could come down to Louisville.[261]

As clear as the choice of Olmsted might have been to Cowan, he would still have to convince the Board of Park Commissioners. And he needed Olmsted's help to do that.

Cowan closed with a plea for haste "as there is very considerable pressure on the Commissioners to appoint an ordinary civil engineer."[262] Indeed there had been. The friends of Clarence Parsons, a city engineer with ambitions of landscape architecture, had been pushing hard for his appointment on grounds of localism—Why hire a Yankee when a hometown man could do the job? The Board was not even willing to officially invite Olmsted to make a pitch.[263]

So Cowan kept his fellow commissioners in the dark; they knew nothing of his letter to Olmsted. Soon it would be clear that his secrecy was warranted.[264]

As for Olmsted, the old man was not in the habit of turning good work down, no matter how busy he already was. He assumed Louisville would be added to his firm's already extensive portfolio of ongoing projects.[265]

Cowan had to remind Olmsted in a second letter that Louisville was not a done deal. "We stand in need of advice which we cannot very well wait for until you might be able to visit us in February," he wrote. Most urgent was the question of what to do with Jacob Park and the other existing park land. Evidently, the Board was considering selling the Jacob Park to cut its losses, even though the state's authorizing legislation had explicitly required them to keep it.[266]

Cowan added a less-than-veiled threat that the work could go to someone else. "If you will… state when you could come to give us advice, if at all," he wrote, "and at the same time will recommend another Landscape Architect, as you suggest, to whom we might at once apply for advice in case that it seems impracticable to wait for you, I shall lay the Communication before the Board with out delay."[267]

Cowan's ploy worked. Within a month, Olmsted dispatched Codman from the Exposition madness to spend a few days in Louisville. With Commissioners Cowan, Castleman, Durrett, and Board President Sherley attending, Codman went to Jacob Park, the waterworks northeast of town, and to another potential site along the city's western bank. Finally, the Commissioners asked for an official proposal from the Olmsted firm.[268]

Codman sent a report to Olmsted, who was back at the firm's headquarters in Brookline, Massachusetts: "The work as it stands there today is in many respects in pretty bad condition," he wrote. Especially at Jacob Park, "which had been bought by the former Mayor of the city at a cost of about $25 per acre; and [which] he had improved, as he called it, at a cost to the city of $100,000 more." The so-called boulevards were almost impassible; the money had been wasted, the outlook was bleak. Codman considered telling the Park Commission to abandon whole thing.[269]

But he knew they could never do that. The city had already sunk far too much money to let it go. Codman knew they were stuck with Jacob Park and all its scars. He thought they could at least make some mitigating changes to the steep road.[270] Besides, "the wood is principally oak and beech, and much of it is in good condition and well worth preserving," he told his boss.[271]

As for the commissioners themselves, Codman thought Cowan "will be a particularly valuable man and he seems to have the best interests of the city at heart. Three of the other men whom I met also seem to be of the right sort." Sherley, the board president, however, was "a politician in the truest sense, and his one idea now seems to be to propitiate everybody to get himself elected to Congress."[272]

On the whole, Codman was impressed with the Park Commission. "What they have in mind there," he wrote, "is something much more ambitious than simply the development of this one tract. They are contemplating a complete system of parks, which shall include land in the three divisions of the city: south, west, and east." Codman thought they could use roads reserved for light traffic to connect the eastern and western parks, similar to the "parkways" Olmsted had used in Buffalo.[273]

"Of course it would be necessary for you to go there personally sometime this Spring," Codman told his boss.[274]

Six days later, the Olmsted firm sent their official proposal to Sherley. They offered to examine the grounds more thoroughly and offer preliminary advice, and if that advice was satisfactory to the Board, they would then spend 1-3 years preparing the full plans for the park system at a rate of $12.50 ($314.50 in today's dollars) per acre.[275]

"Gentlemen," Cowan replied, "I have heard opinions expressed which lead me to think that your proposal will not be accepted in its present shape, but if you can see your way to modify it so far as to name ten dollars an acre instead… I believe that it will go through when presented to the Board."[276]

Once more, Cowan was writing on his own behalf—not representing the Board. Perhaps, strictly speaking, he shouldn't have been writing at all, at least not with inside information that would give the Olmsted firm a better chance of winning the contract. But Cowan wanted them.

"I am anxious that you should receive the Contract because I think it for the best interests of the City to secure your services," he told the firm.[277] Olmsted's personal visit, Cowan thought, would seal the deal.

Nine days later, Sherley sent a letter to the firm office in Brookline. "I was instructed, he wrote on behalf of the Board, "to ask you to let us know the earliest date at which you could come here…. We now have elegant weather and the people are urging us to select the grounds and improve those we have, and I trust that your Mr. Olmsted will be able to come at once."[278]

It was around this time that Cowan acquired the options for the lovely McFerran and Griswold woods and the McFerran and Bonnycastle and Cochran and Barret land.

He still hadn't told his fellow commissioners a word about them. The Board was new; Cowan didn't know whom he could trust. That was why Harry Codman had visited the waterworks site northeast of town, instead of these lovely woods along Beargrass Creek.

Finally, Cowan decided to tell the other Republican on the Board, E.C. Bohne. To Cowan's astonishment, Bohne declined to support him. For one thing, Bohne thought the scheme was too expensive. For another, Bohne lived in the West End and wanted as good a park for that part of town as Cowan was planning for the East End. With $100,000 already pledged to cover Jacob's expenditures on Burnt Knob, there would be little left for a western park if Cowan's wishes were fulfilled.

"Besides," Bohne told him, "I am committed to the purchase of the Schwartz Woods, with about ten or eleven acres adjoining, owned by Col. Castleman. He asks about three times its value, but even then the Schwartz Woods and Castleman's land would cost vastly less than yours, and certainly as much as we could expend for the Eastern Park."[279]

Cowan was speechless. He pleaded with Bohne to give him time to negotiate the asking prices down and then set off to see John McFerran, who alone owned 250 of the acres along Beargrass Creek.

Cowan explained his plan to McFerran, along with Bohne's opposition. Cowan thought if he could raise $20,000 in private money to supplement the Board's allowance, not only would Bohne relent but Sherley and the new mayor, Henry Tyler (who also had a seat on the Board) could be persuaded, and thus the Schwartz Woods plan would be blocked.

"Where do you expect to get the money?" McFerran asked him.

"Well, I thought you would give ten thousand dollars," Cowan replied. McFerran, after all, stood to benefit greatly from a large public park adjoining his property.

"I will," said McFerran. "Who are you going to levy on next?"

"Mrs. Bonnycastle is working herself to death to pay interest on a big mortgage," Cowan told him. "I am going to ask her to subscribe three thousand, and then I shall ask Mrs. Barrett to give two thousand, and then I shall tackle Bill Ray, who is President of a Company that has bought a good deal of land on New Broadway, running back north quite aways, for five thousand." He added that the park would be a "bonanza" for Ray's land company.[280]

Together, Cowan and McFerran went to Mrs. Bonnycastle, who indeed pledged $3,000. A few days later, Cowan got the $2,000 from Mrs. Barrett, but only succeeded in getting $1,000 from Ray.

No matter; Cowan's $16,000 in new money was enough to satisfy Bohne, who switched sides, supporting Cowan's plan over Castleman's.[281]

Colonel Castleman was out of town when Cowan flipped Sherley and Tyler, and so put the last nails in the plan to buy Castlewood.

To reach Sherley, Cowan led two of their mutual friends on a hike through the valley of Beargrass Creek. He showed them the beautiful woods, the rocks, the creek, the wildlife. All of this could belong to the people if only they would exercise Cowan's options. Cowan asked them to buttonhole Sherley at the train station the next morning, when the latter returned from Iowa, and get his support on the spot.

To reach Mayor Tyler, Cowan enlisted their mutual friend Thomas Speed. After briefing Speed on the unbelievable land options versus the Schwartz Woods scheme, Cowan asked Speed to go to Tyler's house that night and secure a promise of support. Speed did as Cowan asked, but the mayor wouldn't commit one way or the other.

Cowan slept fitfully. It was Thursday; the next Board meeting wasn't until the following Tuesday.

When Tuesday finally came, all the Commissioners were present—all

except for Castleman. Cowan pitched his idea for the McFerran and Griswold woods and the surrounding land and told the Board about the options
he'd secured. Then he made a motion for the Board to activate the options
and buy the land. Bohne seconded. One commissioner expressed reserva-
tions—the land titles might not be clean; the Board could spend money on
land they might not end up owning; due diligence would require a full title
examination by attorneys.

"Gentlemen, I will guarantee the titles," Cowan responded.

"Colonel Cowan, I think you are taking a great risk," said Mayor Tyler.

"I don't think so Mr. Mayor, but regardless of personal risk, I promise to
guarantee the titles, and I beg you all to accept the options tonight, for it may
be too late tomorrow."

Sherley, the Board president, put Cowan's motion to a vote. It was a
unanimous yes.

Cowan had won—again. He was satisfied. "The Board had now acquired
the most desirable Park site in Jefferson County," he said.[282]

Three months later, Olmsted rode with Harry Codman across the inter-
minable flat of Indiana on a clattering train bound for Louisville. He spent a
lot of time on trains like this, and it was wearing on him.[283] He was constantly
visiting cities in the Northeast, the Midwest, and now the South. Why? Why
at his age, with his miserable health, was he doing this? Because, as he told
his old friend Fred Kingsley, it was "the part of the work of our practice that I
can least turn over to my partners."[284] After all, Olmsted could see things that
not even Codman, not even his son John, could see. Apparently, that part of
the job couldn't be taught.

Olmsted also made the trips because the firm was running out of Northern cities to work for. The South and the West—they were the firm's future.
Writing from Louisville, he told John, "I want you to be making way in the
sub-tropical and the arid cities before I go. I want the firm to have an established
"good will" at the South."[285] "Very soon, our Northern cities will all have been
provided with parks. Future business in park designing will be in the South."[286]

Olmsted often worried about what would happen to the firm when he was gone. Setting his sons up to succeed him was really the only thing he could think to do for either of them. Also, just 30 years removed from slavery, the South was a place, perhaps more than any other, which needed Olmsted's inclusive philosophy for park design.

And so he rode with Codman through the wheat and corn, with the winds howling across the plains of Merrillville and Lafayette, past Indianapolis, down to the river that separated North from South.[287]

When Olmsted got to Louisville and Cowan showed him the newly-acquired woods along the Beargrass valley, Olmsted was astounded. "I never saw a park in my life which has as many natural advantages as the property just purchased," he said. "If we had such trees about Boston every one of them would be famous."[288]

Really, he could not get over these woods. "The trees are of a splendid quality and beautifully grouped; there is a magnificent supply of fine spring water; the rocks and shrubs are perfect and all in all it is a lovely place naturally."[289] With its mix of woods and meadow and creek, the land was spectacularly well suited for exactly the kind of park Olmsted most liked to plan.[290]

That night, Cowan threw a dinner party at the Pendennis Club for 24 distinguished guests, including a majority of the Board of Park Commissioners.[291] The Pendennis Club (which still exists) was founded two years after the Salmagundi Club, and unlike the Salmagundi Club, it had its own clubhouse—a grey limestone mansion that could seat 150 people at a banquet, such as the one the club had thrown for President Chester Arthur when he came to visit Louisville in 1883.[292] Recently, the Pendennis mansion had been renovated, enlarging the reading room and outfitting it with polished mahogany, and lining the billiards room in antique ivory. They added a separate entrance for women.[293] The club had its own chef,[294] well versed in haute cuisine and a staff that kept the house stocked with champagne and Old East India sherry.[295]

The first time Cowan had met with his fellow Park Commissioners at the Pendennis Club it hadn't gone so well. The Commission had just been elected, but there still remained the referendum on the Park Act itself. Cowan wanted to go ahead and sort out who among the Commission would be President, who would be Secretary, and so forth. Castleman wanted to wait. "I think it would be premature to organize before the bill is approved," he said. "It would not do to say anything about the officers, but we will have a meeting in a few days to discuss preliminary matters. I want plenty of small parks."[296] And apparently that was that. There was, of course, a particular place where Castleman hoped to see a small park—the place he happened to own.

Perhaps Cowan thought the alcohol would dissipate any remaining resistance the commissioners might have toward Cowan's vision for the park system. And perhaps he thought Olmsted's charisma would take care of the rest.[297]

The Park Commissioners had only a general idea of what they wanted (more or less what Cowan had originally proposed)—a park system, with three large parks, a Grand Boulevard, plus some small parks.[298] A few of them had made an effort to study the park systems of other cities, some of which Olmsted had designed.[299] And some of the sites had already been chosen: the southern park was, for better or worse, already set as Jacob Park; the nucleus of the eastern park would now be the McFerran and Griswold woods; and the western park would be somewhere along the Ohio River along the city's western bank. Beyond that, they were waiting for advice. Olmsted did not disappoint.

"Scenery" was the highest praise in Olmsted's vocabulary. He was an evangelist for scenery.[300] And scenery is what he proposed to Louisville. Scenery, he wrote, would "promote a restful, contemplative and musing disposition of mind." In fact, he said, scenery could be "admired only *with* such a disposition of mind."[301] The emphasis was all Olmsted's.

"If you look for work in a park that will justify the borrowing of the money it will cost," Olmsted told the Louisville Board of Park Commissioners, "it will not be the work that has been designed to attract admiration of itself, but that has been designed as a contribution to something larger and fine. To scenery."[302]

If Louisville was determined to have three parks, he said, they should be complementary rather than duplicative: "Develop within each one of your three properties a treasure of rural and sylvan scenery, of a character distinct from that which you will develop within either of the other two." Building three similar parks would be "as wasteful as three city halls." The entire point of a park system was that no one park needed to be all things to all people.[303]

Olmsted didn't like sports in his parks.[304] He didn't even like statues or ostentatious flowers—which he strenuously lobbied the Commission to avoid. In Olmsted's mind, the best kind of park was one where you forgot you were in a planned space at all. Everything—hills, the plants, the roads—was meant to produce tranquility. This is what distinguished Olmsted's parks from the common pleasure gardens, which could not provide "the healthfully soothing and refreshing effect which experience proves is exercised upon people escaping from the splendor and bustle, the confinement and disturbance of towns, into the midst of spacious natural scenery." Like a cow in the flower garden, every superfluous statue or flowerbed could break the trance of scenery Olmsted worked so hard to create.

Finally, Olmsted encouraged the Commission to ignore, for the time being, how the parks might raise real estate values. "Such habits are apt for a time to impede the exercise of fair and sound judgment."[305] "It would be better that the city have no parks at all for the next hundred years than that it should be saddled with such wretched, make-shift, incoherent parks as would result if it should be attempted to make the business of your Commission, now or hereafter, a business of political bargains and the marketing of patronage."[306] (That Jacob Park so well fit such a description was left unsaid.) These must have been welcome words to the ears of Andrew Cowan, staunch defender as he was against the self-interested proposals that were designed more for profit than parks.

Not everyone was taken with Olmsted and his Cowan-like vision for Louisville (which most likely did not include Castlewood). Sherley and Castleman voted against him.[307]

But Olmsted charmed just enough members of the Board of Park Commissioners.

He was hired.[308]

A month later, in July 1891, Olmsted and Codman stopped in Louisville on their way from Chicago to Biltmore. It was hot. Swamp pervaded the city. Their hotel, the five-story Galt House, lay just up the bank from the waterfront. The river slugged along, brown and slow.[309]

Both men were sick. Olmsted had a bad cold, sweating either from fever or the swamp heat, or both.[310] Codman was even sicker, his fever higher, his condition worse. It may have been a recurrence of malaria, something Olmsted also knew from personal experience.[311] Olmsted was worried about his protégé and sent him home to recuperate (it's not clear if that meant Brookline or Chicago, where Codman had relocated for the Exposition work).

The next day, Olmsted was off to Biltmore. He wouldn't stop worrying until he heard Codman was okay.[312]

By August 1891, Codman was sufficiently recovered to make the trip back to Louisville. He inspected the existing park property, reiterated the need to treat Jacob Park as a forest, and gave a pep talk about the potential for Louisville to establish a great park system.[313] While he was there, a closely divided Park Commission renamed the parks.[314]

Cowan proposed Beargrass Park for the eastern park, Sunset Park for the west, and Forest Hill for the South. The *Courier-Journal* later signaled approval for these names, but it was too late. The majority of the Park Commission voted to give the three large parks American Indian names as a tribute to "the original owners of the soil."[315] The eastern park became Cherokee Park; the yet-to-be-purchased western park became Shawnee Park, and Jacob Park, which, of course, already had a name was rechristened Iroquois Park. Castleman introduced a further resolution to prevent the parks from being named after any living man.[316]

To strip Jacob Park of its Jacob's name was audacious and highly controversial. The very next day the city's Board of Alderman passed a resolution condemning the Park Commission's actions.[317]

But that was fine; the Park Commission was in control.

Chapter 10

The Roads

One of the pleasures of an Olmsted park is the driving. The road comes down the hill, curves enough to pitch your weight, bends sharply back into the valley it once looked down on, and lilts over the stone bridge into the flat bottomland of the creek.

When the leaves are gone, you can really see the bones of the park—the trunks, the branches, the ridges, the hillsides carpeted in moldering auburn leaves. When the ice thaws, water rises through the forest floor. It smells like rain.

The sun sets behind the naked trees. Headlights curl down the hill, around the bend, back into the valley.

Horse-drawn "driving" was a favorite pastime well before the advent of the automobile. Guests would come into town and you would, if you were wealthy, take them on a carriage ride.[318]

The only place Louisville had to drive to was the cemetery.[319] The parks would fix this, if and only if the drives to the parks and within the parks were, to use Olmsted's word, "picturesque."[320] In order to achieve that effect, the roads had to be just right.

Olmsted didn't generally think parks—which were art—could be designed by engineers, who were technicians. In fact, he had spent much of his career fighting against the assumption that run-of-the-mill civil engineers could design parks just as well as he could. "It has invariably occurred, in our experience," he told Andrew Cowan, "that an engineer who has been engaged only in the ordinary run of engineer's work, such as that of railroad, sewers and streets, finds it very difficult to disembarrass"—*disembarrass*—"his mind of the customs of such work and to give due consideration to, and find means of realizing, the requirements of grace, beauty, and naturalness, that are made upon him in the work of parks."[321]

An engineer would see a road as a math problem; Olmsted saw it as a line. A road was a composition, a vehicle in itself, transporting the driver through scenery.[322] "Art," he said, "is vexed by harsh lines."[323] When Olmsted was gone, his graceful lines faded from the firm's work, replaced eventually by running tracks and golf courses. The kinds of lines an engineer *could* draw.

But of course, Olmsted relied on engineers to do much of the implementation of his designs. A good park engineer had to at least understand the art of the parks in addition to the technical aspects of the work.

Louisville needed a chief engineer, who could act as the firm's presence in Louisville while Codman and Olmsted were away. Olmsted insisted on Emil Mahlo, a man who had spent the last two years helping survey and lay out the grounds of Fairmount Park in Philadelphia, and who Olmsted thought possessed "an unusual aptitude for the business."[324]

There was opposition to Mahlo on the usual grounds that he wasn't local. One of the Park Commissioners went so far as to promise the *Courier-Journal* that even though the park architects might be outsiders, the engineers would be local residents as much as possible.[325]

However, Olmsted's endorsement carried a lot of weight, and Mahlo was hired. The first thing the new head engineer did was survey the topography of Iroquois and Cherokee Parks. These would be the foundation of the firm's work.[326]

By November 1891, the gracefully-lined maps were finished and sent to the Olmsted firm.[327]

Over the winter, the park work stalled. The only significant thing that happened in the parks between November and April was the purchase of sheep to mow the meadows of Cherokee Park.[328]

There was a big ravine at the "entrance" to Cherokee Park, which prevented people from getting into the park. That made the people unhappy, which made Cowan and the other Commissioners unhappy.[329] Cowan and the Commissioners kept telling the firm about the ravine problem, but the message had not gotten through. Cowan was usually content to write to the firm in general—"F.L. Olmsted & Co." But in April 1892, he took the step of writing to Codman directly. "We are all being subjected to a great deal of annoyances & criticism about the delay in doing something for opening Cherokee Park,"[330] he told Codman.

And it wasn't just the ravine that Cowan and the Board were trying to move along. There was also a Park Avenue parkway into Cherokee Park, a traffic circle, and more land for Iroquois Park.[331]

"[I] infer that nothing is being done for us at Brookline," Cowan grumbled.[332]

He was right. Nothing was being done for them in Brookline, or Chicago for that matter, at least, nothing much. Codman was buried under the Chicago work. As for Olmsted, he was spent. In addition to his manifold chronic maladies, he had apparently gotten arsenic poisoning from his new Turkish red wallpaper.

Finally, in March, the firm sent a road plan to Mahlo in Louisville and asked him to stake out the roads before Olmsted got there the following week.[333]

Incredibly, this was the moment that Olmsted decided a European vacation was what he needed most. On April 2, 1892, Olmsted left for Liverpool, taking with him his son Rick, his daughter Marion, and Harry Codman's younger brother Phil.[334]

He left his work—all of it—to his lieutenants, Harry Codman and John Olmsted.

Chapter 11

Olmsted in Europe

The weather in England in April 1892 was miserable—snow and wind every day. And yet, being there did wonders for Olmsted's spirits—at first.[335]

He hadn't been to Europe since visiting John, who had studied abroad some fourteen years earlier. Being back made Olmsted nostalgic. He thought of his first time in Europe, of Birkenhead Park, the place where he'd first heard his avocation so many years ago. "I find after the result of forty years rumination of landscape that much as I enjoyed in my first visit I did not nearly understand the country & interest of the country," he wrote to John. "If I could afford it, I would now again go right back on the same ground."[336]

Olmsted returned to Europe as the greatest park architect that the United States had ever or would ever produce. He looked at his surroundings with professional interest. "We have seen within two days," he told John, "large, grovelike bodies of naturally growing yews … –a good deal of English forestry… all instructive for Biltmore."[337]

And, as he had once doubted John's abilities; now he doubted Rick's.[338] "I have enjoyed more and learned more than I anticipated," he wrote to Codman, "against Phil and Rick, because they do not get the full landscape charm and are not moved to truly analyze its constituents." Codman's brother was, in Olmsted's estimation, overly enthralled with the landscapes of great estates—"all a lifeless approximation to a very limited range of patterns, or at the best, ideals.

We see no spark of invention or originality…. there is no more original design in any individual case than in a fashionable hat on the 500th proof impression of a copper plate."[339]

At least Phil showed *some* appreciation for English landscapes; if Rick had any, it was "rather less evident." Olmsted suspected it was because Rick was younger and less educated. Perhaps, he expected his son and namesake, trodding the same ground, to feel the same sense of wonder that Olmsted had felt at the same age in the same place.[340]

As delighted as Olmsted was with England, he was unimpressed with France. "There is nothing attractive or good in what is now to be seen in the grading of the Tuilleries," he wrote to Harry and John. "The shrub planting is poor, confused, underdesigned." Even Manning, the firm's horticultural-ist, "would do much better without special instructions." In fact, Olmsted complained, they had "seen no landscape architecture" in northern France "in natural style of modern design. It is all designed bit by bit, theatrically and without connection or breadth of unity."[341] Thinking of the Columbian Exposition, he added, "the less we think of Paris examples, I am inclined to think the better will be the results."[342]

Back in Louisville, Harry Codman uncovered a scheme to connect two hills—one inside Cherokee Park and one outside of it—with a 120-foot tall electric rail bridge.[343] "It is somewhat difficult to explain," the firm wrote, but it was important to prepare "the minds of visitors gradually and uncon-sciously, as they pass from the entrance to the hill, for the fullest enjoyment of the Park."[344] A tall bridge would ruin that effect. "If they pass over a foot-bridge 120 feet high, it is to be feared that most [visitors] would find the Park scenery comparatively tame after the exhilarating effect of the bird's eye views from such a dizzy height."[345]

Thomas Sherley agreed with the firm about the 120-foot-bridge—it *was* a bad idea (eventually, the ravine would simply be filled; problem solved).[346] But more important to Sherley was *how* did the firm get that information? Who was Harry Codman talking to? Whoever it was, he was outside the official channels. "I would," Sherley wrote to the firm, "respectfully suggest that matters that are talked of on the outside, and which may be communicated to you from unofficial sources (and when I say unofficial, I mean in all cases except when under the signature of the President or the Secretary of the Board, or the Chairman of some of the standing Committees, authorized by the Committees to ask for or to furnish such information) that you do not give them any official notice, and I would respectfully suggest that the expression of opinion from individual members of the Board is entitled to equal consideration from your firm."[347]

So it seems Sherley had found about Cowan's constant, often effective, ex parte communications with the Olmsted firm. In fact, Sherley was insecure about it. He hadn't wanted to hire Olmsted in the first place, and now he didn't want Olmsted getting information from anyone but him. But Cowan had a special relationship with the Olmsted firm, which gave him more power than his position would indicate. That was a simple fact—a fact that helped Louisville immensely, even if it didn't always help Sherley personally.

Even Cowan didn't always get his way with the Olmsted firm. In May, Cowan and Mahlo sent Harry Codman a telegram suggesting how the road from the Alexander estate should run—along the corner of the Barringer line, along the ridge "between the two sink holes. This will avoid filling low ground just north of the Barringer line road to the right."[348] "We have considered the matter carefully," the firm replied, "and beg to report that while the line of the road suggested by Mr. Cowan would be an excellent one in many respects considered by itself, and would… save breaking into the fine hillside, it cannot be considered as an alternative to the piece of road for which he proposes to substitute it, because it does not serve at all the same purpose."[349]

Codman, meanwhile, was sick again and had gone back to Brookline.[350]

Olmsted was on the European continent for almost two months, and then returned to England. He was glad to be back in a land of "common plants," away from the frippery and formalism of France, and drove around the countryside gathering inspiration, and dozens of suggestions for Codman.[351]

It was a relief to Olmsted that he'd left the firm business in such capable hands. He planned to be back in the States about June 16th, when he could resume his place at the head of the Chicago work and check in on his various other projects, including Louisville.[352]

And then he was flattened by depression. The day Olmsted was supposed to be back in America, he sent Codman a letter from Hampstead, England, just north of London, where he was staying with a doctor friend. "Dear Harry, You know that I am practically in prison here," he wrote.[353] Though he grumbled about his "prison keeper" doctor, Olmsted admitted the man was doing all he could. There was simply nothing to be done but wait patiently. Of course, that had never been Olmsted's strong suit. "Every day I look for a decided improvement and thus far every day I am disappointed," he told his protégé. "I am only to have you as well informed as I can."

As much as possible, Olmsted tried to make it a working recovery. He asked Codman to catch him up on their many projects. "I should like the briefest reference to your progress not only at Chicago… but at Louisville, Marquette, Reid's, Twombly's, and Newport."[354]

He was a restless convalescent. After overexerting himself at a large park, Olmsted rested by driving through two smaller parks. "There has been little for us to learn in them, except what to avoid. We have photographs."[355] He engaged his son Rick and a friend named George Glessner to conduct a photographic survey of the Hampstead area. "They will have taken, I suppose near a hundred photographs, chiefly of modern small villas and cottages, entrances, lych gates, ivy hung walls, bridges, stables, inns, churches, and roadside matters."[356] He also went with Phil Codman to Hyde Park and Regents Park on "reconnaissance."

He hoped to leave in two or three days for New York. But, by the end of the July he had only made it as far as Chislehurst. In fact, he wouldn't make it back to Chicago until October.[357]

If there was a bright spot, it was that Olmsted was growing more optimistic about Rick's progress. "Rick is getting a familiar acquaintance with picturesque scenery that should be of much value to him," he wrote to John, "& though he is very boyish & thoughtless, in a way, as I was at his age, the habit of looking at matters he is passing with an eye to photographing, if nothing else, compels a more exact kind of observation than he would otherwise use."[358]

The trip had been a success in other ways, too. Olmsted was more sure now than ever that his shop was designing better landscapes than anyone anywhere. "There is much less art of design in landscape in England & France than in Brookline," he wrote to Codman. He was itching to get back to it. "I assume that soon after my return it will be desirable—extremely desirable—that I should take a very long [railroad] journey, Rochester, Chicago, Louisville, Kansas City, Biltmore, Atlanta, and various places."[359]

In August 1892, the Louisville Board of Park Commissioners promoted John Breckinridge Castleman to the presidency.[360] In one of his first official acts as board president-elect, Colonel Castleman donated a wild turkey to Cherokee Park. The minutes reflected that it was a "fine specimen… domesticated."[361] Cowan motioned to accept the turkey of the president-elect, and the Board adopted the motion unanimously.

A little later in the meeting, Castleman proposed installing a double-row hedge of Osage orange* "splashed with 5 wires" around the borders of Iroquois and Shawnee Parks. Again, Cowan moved to adopt Castleman's resolution, pending the approval of the Olmsted firm.[362]

The firm's response bordered on contempt: "The Osage Orange hedge referred to is an excellent one for the use of farmers, but it is entirely unsuitable for enclosing a park," John wrote to Cowan. He used the word "unsuitable" three times in six sentences.[363] Instead, he told Cowan, the parks would be bordered with "dense groves of trees."[364] Indeed, that was a key part of the Olmsted design—dense trees along the border to screen out the outside world. It was a park, not a cow pasture.

Castleman, apparently ignorant of John's flat rejection of the Osage hedge, wrote to the firm three days later, and directly proposed that very thing. He

---

* A sinewy medium-sized tree that showers inedible green fruits in the fall.

asked for the firm's opinion as soon as practicable.[365] John's response to this was even more biting—something to the effect of "how about barbed wire instead?"[366] But John's sarcasm seemed to roll off Castleman's back like rain on the feathers of a (domesticated) wild turkey. "The barbed wired fence recommended by you presents the objection of being cruel," he chastised John. Unacquainted as he was with the fundamentals of park planning, Castleman had a hard time understanding why Osage orange was inappropriate. "I beg to advise that your expression in relation to the Osage orange hedges is entirely at variance with that personally made by Mr. Codman during a recent visit to Louisville." Besides in Castleman's own experience, they were wonderful.[367]

Perhaps Castleman had misunderstood Codman (which seems plausible). Or, if Codman had indeed signaled approval for the hedge, perhaps it had been a rare mistake, excusable given the health problems he'd been having. Or, perhaps he was simply saying yes to the new president now, knowing John could play the heavy later. As one of the designers of the groves of trees along the border, it would be exceedingly unlikely for Codman to seriously consider the Osage orange hedge.

But what to make of Andrew Cowan's support of these ideas? He may have simply exercising his strong political instincts to get on the new president's good side, letting the firm play bad cop, letting them tell Castleman no. After all, he hadn't gotten this far by provoking powerful people unnecessarily.

A month later, still in Chislehurst, Olmsted was finally ready to come home. He arranged for John to meet him in Boston, so he could head to Chicago as soon as possible. "I shall be ready to go unless I am the worse for the voyage."[368] Of course, when he finally, finally arrived home, he was worse for the voyage. In fact, he told John, he felt worse than he had before he ever left for Europe.[369]

And yet, when Olmsted got back to Chicago at the beginning of October, Harry Codman was again, remarkably, the sicker of the two men. The cause of his suffering was a recurring stomach pain.[370] Once again, he recovered well and was soon back on the job.[371]

Cowan had been eager for Olmsted's return. The old man had sway with the other Commissioners that could not easily be replaced. Cowan thought they needed more land for Cherokee Park, but he wanted that message to come from Olmsted, not from him or Mahlo. Sherley had opposed buying even the Barringer land, "although it was indispensible, as I thought," Cowan wrote, and had become "the main entrance to Cherokee Park." Now Sherley was opposing the purchase of ten additional acres for Cherokee Park and yet wanted the Board to buy a square of land for a small park elsewhere. "We haven't enough money to pay for it," Cowan harrumphed, "yet he sticks to the thing, for reasons that need not be mentioned here."[372]

Cowan's main concern was that if Mahlo crossed Sherley, even on behalf of the Olmsted firm, the engineer would damage his own standing.[373]

Cowan had also wanted John, who had been so effective at vetoing bad ideas in his father's absence, to accompany the patriarch on a planned visit in September—a visit that had not happened for either man, due to Olmsted's prolonged recovery.[374]

Olmsted's health was still bad. He was "tortured with neuralgia and toothache," he told John. What's more, he couldn't shake his sense of unease. "I am tired," he wrote John, "and have a growing dread of worry & anxiety." It was a steady, quickening drumbeat in his mind.[375]

In October, Codman suggested to his partners that the firm might benefit from opening a western branch office—a region that would include Louisville. Olmsted was giving it some thought. It made sense, with Olmsted's vision of the West as the firm's future. With Codman in Chicago for the World's Fair, the firm effectively had a western branch already, but when Exposition wrapped up, he and Codman would no longer have a convenient perch from which to set out for Louisville, Milwaukee, and Kansas City. A western office would also allow room for more partners to join the firm rather than risk losing talented staff in need of promotion.

Characteristic of Harry Codman, it was a damned good idea.[376]

Codman even weighed in on Louisville projects that were technically being executed by other firms.

On both ends of Market Street, east and west, the width of the street bulged to five lanes wide, wide enough to accommodate the stalls of the farmers and hawkers and slaughterers who had gathered there regularly for decades. Beginning in 1890, the market squares were repurposed. Lutz wrote to the Park Commission and suggested they take over the projects. They agreed and brought in the architecture firm of McDonald & Bro. Harry Codman gave advice on behalf of the Olmsted firm.

The team created Kenton Place and Logan Place—slivers of parks in the middle of the road, running the length of most of the block, taking three of the five lanes of Market Street. Two—the outer lanes—were rows of symmetrical trees. Tree screens in miniature. There were fountains in the centers. And at Logan Place, an arbor was built over the fountain, complete with shaded benches. You could sit on them and almost forget you were right in the middle of a busy road.[377]

The city removed the parks for the streetcar just a few years later. Eventually, the streetcar also vanished, leaving nothing but a road five lanes wide at either end, haunted by the ghosts of its parks and markets.

In November, Castleman again wrote to the firm with a new idea. He wanted to damn up Beargrass Creek and create a lake. "I am quite sure that public sentiment will demand this, and believe it can be done without great cost and in a manner to be made almost as beautiful as your construction at Buffalo Park," he told the firm. Enclosed was a drawing by Mahlo of where the lake could lie.

Codman and John Olmsted both read the letter. Their reply is lost. Eventually, though, there would be a small lake on the northern boundary of the park.

In January, Harry Codman went to the hospital. As it turned out, he had appendicitis; he'd had it for months. He had surgery, which was successful. His recovery was supposed to be slow, though he would be out of the office in the few crucial months before the grand opening of the Columbian Exposition.

And then, unexpectedly, he died.[378] His brilliant mind shut down, never to design landscapes again.

Olmsted was devastated. "You will have heard of our great calamity," he wrote to his colleague Gifford Pinchot in Asheville. "I am as one standing on a wreck and can hardly see when we shall get afloat again."[379]

Indeed, in many ways, he never did.

The death of a partner so competent, so vital, key to so many business enterprises as Codman would have thrown almost anyone into the dark. But Olmsted? As worn down as he already was? This could be the end.

The old man sat at Codman's desk, looking at the stacks of papers and memoranda.[380] It was overwhelming. After a few days, though, he could start to see a way forward.[381] Clearly, without Codman, they could not do as much as before. Olmsted wanted the firm to shed its less important business. He told John to be "thoroughly respectful," to their clients in the Kirkwood neighborhood project in Atlanta, but to inform them that "owing to my illness and Mr. Codman's death they cannot depend on our advancing their work before any given near day. If they wish our resignation under these circumstances, they can have it." For emphasis, he underlined, "let it plainly appear that <u>we would prefer to be relieved of a duty that we cannot once feel sure of meeting to their satisfaction.</u>"[382]

But really, Olmsted could not bear to jettison most of his projects. Chicago, Biltmore, and Louisville—these would stay.[383]

The firm quickly added a new partner, Charles Eliot, who had apprenticed for Olmsted at the same time as Harry Codman and had solid credentials as a Harvard graduate who had been running his own landscape practice in Boston.[384] Eliot was a bandage covering the gaping hole left by Codman's death. Regardless of his credentials, Eliot would face a steep learning curve in Chicago and Louisville. And Olmsted had little faith in the health of his soon-to-be partner. "Eliot has a weak constitution with proclivities to lung trouble and in our first conversation said he must look out for his own health," he told John (and indeed, Eliot would die just four years later from meningitis).[385]

Still, it was the only thing Olmsted could do. The firm changed its name to Olmsted, Olmsted, & Eliot in March 1893.[386]

They would move forward—for now.

CHAPTER 12

THE THIRD PARK

Andrew Cowan wore out a horse riding across the length and breadth and the height of the parks—a Standardbred mare and two good buggies, exhausted. He was wearing himself out, too. The park work had become his day job; he ran the leather business at night.[387]

From the beginning, Andrew Cowan had envisioned three parks. The Salmagundi Club had endorsed and promoted three parks. The Olmsted firm was contracted to design three large parks (among other things). And yet, so far there were only two.

The third park had always been planned for west Louisville, and the obvious place to put a park in west Louisville was along the Ohio River, which cut the city off at the pass so that really there is no such thing as northwest Louisville—there is only the river, and beyond the river, Indiana. The Ohio River could be a beautiful, dramatic setting for a park.

But in quite literal sense, Shawnee Park was shortchanged. The Park Commission was originally supposed to issue $1 million in bonds, but due to a dispute with the Sinking Fund Commission the Park Commission ended up with just $600,000, of which only two-thirds could be spent on acquiring park lands. Most of that $400,000 was spent on Cherokee Park; some of it was spent on Boone Square—an existing smaller park in the city interior; so that by the time the western park was acquired, only $122,000 remained.[388]

As with the other parks, there were several different possibilities being put forth by interested parties. There was some land along the river north of Market Street. But Cowan pointed out that much of the land was riverbottom and he'd seen it flood enough for a steamboat to sail right over it. Another group proposed their land along the river south of Broadway. Again, Cowan pointed out a fatal flaw—in this case, a large sewer outflow located just upriver from the land, which would mean swimming in the river would be swimming in sewage.[389]

Cowan's preferred location was in between, stretching from Broadway to a place called Fontaine Ferry Park. Altogether, he saw about 140 acres of land safe from river overflow, spared of sewage outflows, with trees, meadows, and good views of the river.

The owners of this land, many of whom had built country houses with these nice views and meadows in mind, were not eager to part with it. The Park Commission would have to buy them out and pay for the houses just to tear them down.[390]

Another disadvantage Shawnee Park had in being the third park was that expectations had been raised by what had transpired with the previous two parks. And so the landowners held out for more money.[391]

One of the farms was owned by Mr. and Mrs. Blankenbaker, who had just built a nice house there. "Colonel Cowan, I was born on the river and I shall die on the river," Mrs. Blankenbaker declared. "No use to talk any more to me." Cowan evidently passed her comments on to Olmsted, who dryly replied that "the difficulty was not insurmountable," and advised Cowan to tell Mrs. Blankenbaker, "who was not young, that the Board would agree to let her live in the house the rest of her life if she wished, on payment of rent equivalent to six percent on the amount to be paid her for the land on which the house stood, and a few acres of beech grove surrounding it."[392]

Cowan got the option on the Blankenbaker land.[393] Still, some of the remaining landowners were unwilling, causing the Park Commission to pass a resolution authorizing a jury to condemn the land.[394]

It seems that the threat of eminent domain was enough to convince the holdouts to sell, but the progress in establishing the western park had nonetheless been delayed.[395] The land purchase was not finalized until early 1892, about the time Olmsted left for Europe. Finally, in September 1892, the Olmsted firm got the topographical maps, by November, they had submitted their proposal.[396]

The firm's proposal was likely written either by Harry Codman or John Olmsted. The vision it contained was, in some ways, a departure from Olmsted's philosophy—a relaxation of the dogma of quiet in favor of recreation—in a way that would presage the firm's work after the old man was gone. The firm laid out how each park should be different: Iroquois was "great natural forest"; Cherokee—with its "moderately gently-rolling country, with somewhat scattered, broad-spreading trees and a picturesque, small river"—was essentially the Louisville equivalent of Birkenhead Park. But Shawnee—the western park—wasn't like the other two parks. It was flat, it was smaller, it was along the river. It could offer things the other two parks could not. Shawnee could be the "great public common," and "the central play-ground" of the city, where children could play ball in the meadows, where military parades could traipse about and large public gatherings could assemble. The plantings could be more formal, more ornamental, principally used to screen out the outside world and to highlight the views of the river.[397]

The Board gave its assent to the plan in December 1892 and ordered work to begin at once. Perhaps in a sign of the more relaxed times, the Board even allowed an ostrich to be donated to the park.[398]

In February 1893, Olmsted finally returned to Louisville. He brought with him Eliot and Warren Manning, the firm horticulturalist.[399]

It was probably at this time that Cowan took Olmsted to Shawnee Park and showed him the river, which overflowed on the Indiana side but not the Louisville side. Olmsted was impressed. "Colonel Cowan, although you only have one hundred and twenty-five acres for the Park, above high water, or danger of overflow, you have equal to a thousand acres or more for landscape effect," he said.[400]

Two weeks later, the firm submitted its first planting plan for Cherokee Park.[401] There were all the classic Olmstedisms—the graceful lines, the natural feel brought about by meticulous planning, the groves of trees. The firm ordered hundreds of trees from nurseries near and far. There would be silver beech groves and solitary maples bright in the fall. Hawks would cry from the poplars and owls would hoot in the darkness of the bur oaks.[402]

It would be a masterpiece of scenery, Olmsted's highest ideal.

Work proceeded in Louisville over the summer. Under Manning's direction, trees were planted along the borders of all of the parks. A bridge was built in Shawnee, as were two shelters and a house for the ostrich and some peacocks.[403] Southern Parkway, which led from the city to Iroquois Park was finally opened to the public. Sheep were purchased for Cherokee Park and two wood bridges were built over Beargrass Creek.[404]

Eliot visited Louisville alone on April 24th and wrote Olmsted a telegraph "indicating trouble," though what kind Eliot didn't say.[405] Then, from Chicago, Eliot wrote Castleman a five-and-a-half page assessment of the next steps for the park work, most of which focused on smallish details.[406]

Olmsted's new partner—no doubt still trying to find his feet in Chicago—was sending Castleman the message that the firm was at the tiller.

CHAPTER 13

OLMSTED AT THE END

Olmsted's long decline would soon approach its end with the churning speed of a boat long at sea, grounding suddenly on the shoals.

In May, he had been awarded a Doctor of Laws from Harvard University—in many ways a pinnacle of professional recognition for someone who had never gone to college.[407] And yet, he was despairing again soon enough.

Moreover, he was beginning to evidence something new in his long career—insecurity. He began to defer more and more to John. Whatever faith he had once lacked in his adopted son's abilities (and what long and trying years those must have been for John, who, after all, had lost his father and could then never seem to please his famous, difficult stepfather) Olmsted had now in abundance. He deferred to John the final judgment of whether he should make another trip to Chicago and Louisville. "Eliot writes as if you did not think it necessary that I should go to Louisville & Chicago. Let me hear from you distinctly," he wrote to John.[408] "It seems to me highly desirable that I should go to Chicago… I feel this to be a necessity… and if I am going to Chicago… I might not fail to visit Louisville at least."[409] But then if he visited Chicago and Louisville it would be rude to leave off Milwaukee. And if he passed by Rochester (likely on the way from Chicago back home to Boston), he might as well stop for a visit. The same went for Detroit and Buffalo.[410] "I shall be glad if you can persuade me to think otherwise, for I dread the journey

& expense," he told John.[411]

This is how Olmsted's itineraries ballooned to something a man of his health should never undertake. Even more than 120 years later, you can almost feel the anxiety spiraling upward in Olmsted's mind as he thought of more and more things he had to do. Olmsted knew he must go on these journeys—of course he must—and that not just he but also Manning and Eliot, so they might know enough to take over Olmsted's work in the event of his death, an event he contemplated frequently.[412] If Codman could die so young, so healthy, surely Olmsted—now 72—would not be far behind.[413]

Another complicating factor was that Olmsted remembered almost nothing about Louisville. Evidently, much of what was known about the firm's work in Louisville had died with Harry Codman. "It is so long since I have been at Louisville that I shall be lost there if I go alone," he wrote to John. "You must send me the names of the people whom I shall need to render acquaintance with. At this moment, I cannot recall one. At Chicago, they seem to have got away from me."[414]

A month later, he wrote to John again with the same complaint: "Manning & I have not between us sufficient knowledge of the situation at Louisville, & of our office in relation to Louisville, to make it desirable that we should meet the present Board."[415]

This was more than the usual forgetfulness of someone with a hectic schedule. Indeed, though he had little time to wander the woods anymore, Olmsted was getting more lost every day.[416] Winter was creeping in.

It was becoming increasingly clear that not only was Olmsted overworked—which had been true for essentially his entire career—but that he was no longer able to keep up with the workload. In addition to shepherding the massive landscape effort of the Chicago World's Fair Chicago, Olmsted was also heavily involved in planning the grounds of George W. Vanderbilt's mountain château, Biltmore. The latter projected seems to have been Olmsted's personal favorite. In fact, Biltmore had been really the only project where Olmsted had made himself the pointman, in the way Codman had been for

Chicago and Louisville. "This is a place & G.W.V. is a man that we must do our best for," he told John.[417]

In early 1894, he once again was trying to get up to speed on Louisville in advance of a visit. To Eliot, he wrote, "I am culpably ignorant of the condition of things at Louisville, not having kept the run of correspondence as I should. I don't know whether matters have been advanced there at all since our visit… Please give me what information and advice you can."[418]

In a postscript, he added that Phil Codman had found the names of the commissioners, and Olmsted thought he might be able to carry himself decently "except from the quaint dignity and decorum of the President," he said, referring to Castleman.[419]

In March 1894, Olmsted went back to Louisville. The weather was unseasonably warm. Storms rolled in and the rain poured down.[420] "It is a critical moment," he wrote to John, but "[w]e are getting on pretty well here… Have been over two parks today. Shall finish and meet the Board tomorrow night."[421]

Two days later, having met with the Board, and having slept little afterwards, Olmsted wrote to John again. The weather and his health may have been gloomy, but Olmsted was happy. The trip was a success. "I reported at length and with satisfactory results. Matters are in better shape than ever before," he wrote.[422]

His mood wouldn't last. Two days later, he complained to Eliot from New York, "Not only at Atlanta but at Chicago, Louisville, and Brooklyn, I feel that I have been taking on rather appalling loads for the warm weather."[423]

Apparently Olmsted wasn't the only one worrying about his fitness for the job. His partners had been discussing it, too. That summer, Eliot wrote to Olmsted from Brookline, ostensibly to reassure Olmsted about the firm's ability to withstand John taking a vacation. But then, Eliot's letter took a turn for the… Presumptuous? Disloyal? Patronizing? "We both feel," he wrote, with "both" meaning himself and John, "that as this business is chiefly your creation your share should continue to be much the largest."[424] This was Olmsted's most junior partner promising not to cut his pay.

Eliot continued, assuring Olmsted "that so long as you feel poor in health that you ought not to attempt any work or feel any anxiety—except for such special cases as you have an interest in of a special sort."[425] In other words, Olmsted needn't worry his little head. "The fact that you stand in the background as head of the firm is, of course, of great value to our joint business, and neither John nor I would wish to have you formally withdraw one day before Fate may compel that event."[426]

What? It was one thing for Olmsted to bemoan his health and plan for a succession. It was quite another for Eliot, who'd only joined the firm the year before, to openly suggest that Olmsted's hold on the reins was slipping, that he should stay on as a figurehead purely for his famous name, and that he might soon die. It seems that Olmsted noticed. First, Europe; then Codman; now this. "I have never been in so long and deep a depression," Olmsted wrote to his friend William Stiles.[427]

He was also upset with how the New York Park Commission had insulted his old colleague Calvert Vaux, of Central Park fame. When Vaux was appointed to the New York Park Commission, a fellow commissioner had, unfairly, demanded to know the scientific name of Rose of Sharon, which Vaux had been unable to provide.[428] This salted an old, old wound of Olmsted's—that landscape architecture, after all his life's work, was still not respected as an art worthy of genius on the order of architecture, painting, and sculpture. It wasn't even esteemed as highly as horticulture. "I don't know what to say," Olmsted wrote to a friend. "It is an official verdict from the most important tribunal in the country against which I have most stood for and most cared for in all my life… in favor of that with which I have been most in contention and of which contention I am wearied almost to death."[429]

"The crowding misfortunes of the moment," he said, "[are] coming upon me with the general smash of the golden bowl."[430]

As his abilities and spirits declined, he poured much of his remaining energy into two increasingly intertwined projects: Biltmore and his 24-year-old son, Rick.[431]

Olmsted wrote to his son, who was recently graduated from Harvard and fresh off a summer surveying internship in the Rocky Mountains, and tried to bolster his interest in pursuing landscape architecture professionally. "You must apprentice yourself to <u>this</u> business…. . I am confident that in the end you will see that I have been right…. . Stick to it. Get the better of your difficulties. Conquer them carefully, as a man. If you cannot see that I am right, exercise faith in me."[432]

He set up an apprenticeship for Rick at Biltmore, where his son could learn about plants from Pinchot. Rick was something less than grateful. "Your letters have indicated a condition of mind and a position in general with reference to your professional education that seems to me most unfortunate and wrong; ill judged; ill-considered," Olmsted wrote to him.[433]

It was as if he was trying to dispense all the last fatherly advice he was capable of before he was no longer capable of it. Even now, he could not quite make the case he wanted; he hoped his ever-diminishing best was enough. "If I could think out and adequately state my position you would agree with me," he told Rick, "but I am so distracted with many difficulties which I am striving to deal with and so near to breaking down that for the present I despair."[434] He advised Rick to make the best of his opportunity at Biltmore, and learn his plants as best he could.

Olmsted became increasingly gloomy. "Rainy weather interrupts work and keeps me in the house," he wrote to his partners. "I am much dissatisfied, concerned, and impatient." Even Biltmore was vexing. "Both Pinchot and Beadle are questioning my important elements of our elaborated arboretum plans."[435]

And then, in 1895, Olmsted's health suddenly dealt him the professional blow he had long dreaded. In a sense he'd made a career of imagination, the wanderings of a fertile mind. Now his mind wandered without him. It was like his house in Brookline, which had forgotten it was a house and had become instead an ivy thicket.

The man who had led the landscape planning of many of the largest, most important, and most beautiful designed landscapes in the country, could no longer remember what he had just been talking about.

In the summer of 1895, when Olmsted composed three identical letters to George W. Vanderbilt, his most important client.[436] Then he confused the layout of the poplars lining the formal entrance to the Biltmore château.[437] "It has today, for the first time become evident to me that my memory as to recent occurrences is no longer to be trusted," he wrote to John.[438] "If Rick had not been with me and had not privately set me right, I should have shown that fact in a flagrant way to Mr. Vanderbilt."[439]

In his realization that he was no longer a reliable business partner, Olmsted was, as ever, analytical. "I try to look at the situation from an outside and impersonal point of view," he wrote, "and so looking at it I see that I ought no longer to be trusted to carry on important business for the firm alone."[440]

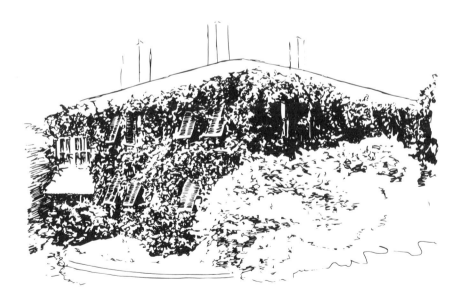

Brookline, Massachusetts home of Frederick Law Olmsted and family

He told John to guard the firm from what harm might result from his mental lapses. Mainly this meant keeping him out of the work.[441]

John made plans to go to Biltmore and collect his stepfather, while Rick would stay behind with Pinchot. George Vanderbilt was in New York but evidently got wind that Olmsted was leaving Biltmore ahead of schedule. "Now please don't," he wrote. "I understood you were going to be at Biltmore all of May... . I have made my plans accordingly and invited Mr. John [Singer] Sargent, the artist, to come to Biltmore May 15th and paint your portrait."[442]

This was somewhat persuasive, and Olmsted stayed for a few more weeks. Sargent started the portrait but he got only the head finished before Olmsted had to leave. Rick put on his father's clothes so Sargent could finish the painting.[443]

The final portrait is perhaps all too accurate. The gentleman landscape architect, is leaning on his cane amidst the rhododendrons. But his eyes are curiously dead. None of Olmsted's sparkle, charm, and intellect come through. The lights had dimmed.

Like Napoleon, Olmsted spent much of his exile on a remote island—in this case, a rocky conifer archipelago off the coast of Maine called Deer Isle. There, he wandered the thorny paths and brambles of his mind—his life like a park big enough to get lost in.

Also like Napoleon, Olmsted did not find it easy to give up the reins. "I am lying awake nights," he told Rick, "in a perplexed state of mind about Biltmore affairs and your professional training, especially in matters of foliage."[444] His letters became increasingly anxious. "I am passing nights in worries of which you might in part relieve me," he told Rick. "For if you told me what I did not like to read, I should like it better than to be worried by vague apprehensions. I want to know more definitely wherein I am not doing my duty, wherein I have blundered, first, toward you, second, toward Mr. Vanderbilt."[445]

Much of the energy Olmsted had until recently devoted to his work, he now devoted to his youngest son. Rick was Olmsted's final project.[446]

"Acquire the habit of... keeping knowledge of the points of a compass when you are pursuing a devious course," he told Rick, "of not getting 'turned around'; of not getting confused in timber, of following a trail, finding springs, and guessing at the basics of water courses, or the means of natural drainage; of seeing by the shape of mountain heights which way streams between them are trending &c &c."[447]

He was almost obsessed with Rick's horticultural acuity. "The troublesome fact now as always remains that we lack a competent head of planting department <u>interested with</u> us, Manning always having divided interest and looking ahead to independence and rivalry rather than intimate cooperation."[449=8] This was the role he saw for Rick in the firm's immediate future, the way he could differentiate himself from John or even from Charles Elliott. Rick didn't get it. So Olmsted kept telling him: "Unless you gain in planting craft at Biltmore you would better have been somewhere else and you will never after make good the deficiency with which you will leave Biltmore."[449]

He ended that letter with ten specific questions he wanted Rick to answer: "Is your health good and sound… ? Are you doing anything and learning anything in forestry? Have you a chance to make any excursions? How are you getting socially?"[450] And so on.

Just a week later, Olmsted wrote Rick a ten page letter in small cursive. He began in a reflective mood. "It is the unavoidable thought of the old man: 'Could I have started with anything like the advantages… that I can give my son, I should have acquitted myself so much better. [Or] 'Let me spare my son the difficulties that I have had.'"[451]

"But," Olmsted acknowledged, "I know that if I had been specially educated and trained for my profession, I should not have been able to try as hard as I did to get the better of my difficulties; should not have been disposed to try. Really, I did go into my work with the spirit of an overardent volunteer; reckless of health; reckless of life, so I could meet my responsibility."[452]

Rick, he knew, would have a different path. "I am always thinking that you will have to make up by deliberate and methodical methods for what you will lack of such impulse ardor and devotion."[453] But "deliberate" and "methodical" didn't seem to be Rick any more than "ardor" and "devotion." And that was what worried Olmsted.

Whatever the doubts, in just a year, Charles Elliot was dead. Rick was brought on as a full partner at just 27 years old, and the firm changed its name to Olmsted Brothers.[454]

"I am still here," Olmsted wrote from Deer Isle in August, "but I can't say that I am enjoying myself."[455]

And by October he was there still. One bright spot was a letter Rick had written to his sister Marion. At night, when he couldn't sleep, Olmsted would light his lamp and read the letter again and again. "Nothing goes as far to lift me out of the feeling of desolation," he told Rick. "It is not childishness. It is the assurance that you are taking up what I am dropping. That and the satisfaction of my affection for you, and I keep writing because I do so wish that I could help you. Yet try as I may, I suppose that I can do nothing materially."[456]

That, really, was the crux of his current depression. The next day he wrote to Rick again. "I try in vain to think of something that I can yet do. I am sure that you do not need advice. You can get yourself better advice that I can offer you."[457] Yet, "I am all the time feeling that I have not done enough for you."[458]

Really, these letters must have been exhausting to Rick. They were incredibly repetitive, paternalistic, micromanaging. Few of Rick's responses survive—if he did respond. John, it seems, had given up. "Give me your impressions," Olmsted implored Rick. "I can get nothing out of John."[459]

"As I am drawn away from [the work] and realize more and more the finality of this withdrawal, intenser grows my urgency to be sure that what I have designed is to be realized," he wrote.[460]

Towards the end of his purgatory, when his thoughts were adrift and his anxieties unmoored and he was under the influence of a prescription of opium, whisky, quinine, and calomel, Olmsted remembered Elizabeth Baldwin, the unrequited love of his youth. Evidently, the pain of her rejection was still there, a lifetime later. Olmsted wrote her a rambling letter on a piece of wrapping paper.[461] "In vino veritas," he sheepishly confessed to his friend Fred Kingsbury.[462]

The former Miss Baldwin, long since Elizabeth Whitney, sent the kind of distant, cordial reply one might expect for an unexpected, untoward reconnection with a short-time fiancé of decades prior.[463] She asked about Olmsted's life, perhaps out of politeness. Olmsted then sent a second letter, fourteen handwritten pages, apologizing for his first letter, but also taking the opportunity to catch up—and, to list his accomplishments. Perhaps he was trying, like Fitzgerald's Gatsby would some 30 years later, to prove that he had been worthy of her hand after all. "I have raised my calling from the rank of a trade, even a handicraft, to that of a liberal profession—an Art, and Art of Design," he told her. "I am thinking that of all the young men that you knew I was the last to have been expected to lead such a life as I have."[464]

Eventually, the Olmsted family decided they could no longer care for their pater familias and placed him in the care of the McLean Hospital in Belmont, Massachusetts. Olmsted had once submitted a design for the grounds, but his vision for them was never carried out. He may still have been cognizant enough to catch the irony, and to be frustrated by what had been done and what had been left undone.[465]

Finally, Olmsted wandered down a path from which he never returned. He died on August 28, 1903. By then, the firm he had founded was well into its second life as Olmsted Bros.[466]

"My dear Olmsted," George Vanderbilt wrote to John, "I see by the papers that the end has come to the sufferings of your invalid [father] and know how peaceful you must feel about it now. These last years have been hard ones for all of you." Writing from Germany, Vanderbilt mourned for "the truly big and loveable nature which has just gone onto the other world."[467] "C'est un grande artiste," wrote Olmsted's French counterpart, Édouard André in a letter of condolence.[468] "Few men have done better service than he," wrote the art professor and public intellectual Charles Eliot Norton, "service beneficent not only to his own generation, but to generation after generation in the long future."[469]

And in Louisville, the Board of Park Commissioners, led by President Castleman, adopted a resolution in Olmsted's memory. "Louisville, starting with his instruction, has, in a little more than a decade, built up a park system which is the admiration of all who know it and which will be more beautiful as his plans are developed," stated the Commission. "We have lost our leader and the country [has lost] one of nature's noblemen, whose place cannot be filled."[470]

"Kindly express our appreciation to the Board," Rick replied. He was one of the men who would now be trying to fill the unfillable place to which Castleman alluded.[471]

CHAPTER 14

AFTER OLMSTED

☙ 1896 ❧

Andrew Cowan looked out at Southern Parkway, and what he saw was beautiful. "At night thousands of bicycles skim over the smooth roadway with their white and red lights flashing and disappearing," he wrote.[472] If they wanted to, these people could ride their bikes all the way from downtown to Iroquois Park and then up the road through the forested hill, to the top where they could see the city glowing with lantern light in the distance.[473]

During the day at Iroquois Park they could hike "the slopes... thickly covered with fine trees," and amble through the "shady groves and open spaces studded with trees." From the top, they could see "the whole length and breadth of the city and fine distant prospects of the beautiful country adjacent to Louisville."[474]

Two electric streetcar lines carried people between the city and Iroquois Park. Another went to Cherokee Park, and one to Shawnee.

From the riverbank of Shawnee Park, "the view, with the deep wooded Indiana 'knobs' beyond the opposite shore, is extensive and beautiful." There were grassy fields, maintained by a flock of sheep, where people could play lawn games. And there was the closest thing Louisville would ever have to a beach, where people could swim and boat on the Ohio River.

Cherokee Park was not the largest park, but Cowan thought it was "the most beautiful."[475] "Its surface is gracefully undulating, and through it flows the middle fork of the famous Beargrass Creek… . Lovers of grand trees, the wide-spreading beech and lofty poplars, stately maples and the black walnut, great oaks and giant sycamores and graceful elms may see them here in native grandeur."[476]

Cowan, who had left the Board of Park Commissioners two years before, had a right to sound satisfied. What had begun as an idea in his head—and what had been, for a time, co-opted and corrupted by politicians and special interests—was now a physical reality shaping the geography and character of the city. Louisville had a functioning park system, open to everyone—all races, all classes—just one year after Olmsted's sudden retirement.

But the work was far from done, and the extent to which the parks were completed as envisioned rested largely on the shoulders of two men: John Olmsted and, increasingly, John Breckinridge Castleman.

John took his father's former roles in Louisville as supervisor, umpire, and artistic authority. As Olmsted had shown, much of the job of a good landscape architect was to say no to bad proposals. And at this, John excelled.

Like his father, John could be thoughtful, explaining with a strong grasp of landscape architecture principles, why an idea wouldn't work, as he had when he shot down the proposal to span the entrance to Cherokee Park with a 120-foot bridge.

But as often as John was thoughtful, he—again, like his father—could be incredibly blunt. In fact, John Olmsted was capable of shooting down the landscape preferences of his own mother with all the grace of a grouse hunt at close range: "You know, of course, that both Rick and I have a very poor opinion of your Deer Isle real estate as an investment," he wrote her.[477] "I cannot help being frank even it if it is disagreeable."

When he* nixed one of Park Commissioner Robert Kinkead's ideas—having a collection of wild birds donated to Cherokee Park—he did not write: "I understand where you are coming from." He did not write: "I know bird collections are very popular." He did not write: "Peacocks are beautiful, but perhaps somewhat distracting to the purpose we are trying to achieve." He wrote, flatly: "Zoological collections are not suitable parts of large rural parks."[478]

When he swatted a high school alumni group's proposal to put a 10-acre arboretum in one of the parks, he told Castleman: "A botanical collection in a rural park would be just as much out of place as a properly qualified and labeled collection of building stones, bricks, terra cotta and other substances used in building would be in or upon a church or city hall."[479]

In all of these ways, John was Frederick Law Olmsted's son and heir. If he felt the burden of now carrying the work of Frederick Law Olmsted without Frederick Law Olmsted, he did not let on. He was clear-eyed in seeing his father as irreplaceable and yet displayed a firm grasp on his role running the firm without the old man.

In fact, what John felt most burdened by in the wake of his father's departure were his mother's plans for Olmsted's care, which included a large house on Deer Isle, complete with two attendants. "Your project simply looks like a scheme to get the house a Deer Isle built that you have been intending to have… It doesn't look like economy somehow. Keeping house in three places for a family of five."[480]

It was interesting to see John playing the aggrieved party. He claimed that his mother only asked his and Rick's advice when it was too late to act on it. "We don't like being dealt with in that sort of way. Then I don't think it was right of you to draw money out of Father's bank [account] with power of attorney to buy land to put in [my sister] Marion's name and my name."[481]

Of course, the Olmsted Brothers were, first of all, brothers. They shared the family drama as well as the family business (Rick even mailed John his underwear from Biltmore).[482] With Rick, John tried to obfuscate how harsh he had been with their mother. "I have written to Mother mildly objecting"— ha!—"to her not consulting us more frankly in regard to the pertinent family matters but cordially supporting her projecting of a home of her own."[483] John's real concern for Deer Isle, he told Rick, was that it was too isolated, too lonely, that their mother would suffer, away from the bustle of Brookline with her famous husband at the epicenter of his world. "She has always been accustomed to a larger family & to agreeable companionship, callers, calling & the like & here she is going to shut herself up with Father & stupid attendants & servants." John thought she would try it for a little while before seeing, as he did, that Deer Isle would not do.[484] "If she had some good natured talkative darky servants it might be some relief, but a solitary white woman servant won't be gay."[485] Oof.

John was unambiguously the senior partner in the Olmsted Brothers. In fact, Rick's earlier promotion to partner had been more of a naming convention than a financial arrangement—understandably, since Rick was still just an apprentice at Biltmore. Now, John laid out the terms of Rick's entry into the practice. He would remain at Biltmore, and could begin taking on firm work to be billed at an hourly rate that would, if full-time, add up to about $33,000 a year in today's dollars.[486]

John also added his own advice to that of their father: "It is better to plan well but talk little. Let our <u>works</u> show."[487]

Already, the Louisville work was facing challenges from the new Board, which in early 1896 fired the Olmsted firm's chosen for park engineer, Emil Mahlo. Newly sworn commissioner Robert Kinkead wrote to the firm, swearing "perfect loyalty to your firm in every particular, and to be perfectly frank with you… we feel certain you will be with us."[488] Having discharged his politeness, he proceeded to stomp on the firm's prerogative. "Know that Mr. Mahlo was your choice, and realizing that you are under the impression that his discharge was only temporary, it is proper that I should say that his reappointment or election is impossible, and therefore in answering this letter you can treat that much as settled."[489] In the postscript, Kinkead added that he'd sent the letter to Castleman.[490]

Whether because of the Mahlo dealings or whether because he needed to visit anyway, John made his third trip to Louisville. While still in town, he wrote, to Castleman. "We have good reason for believing that Mr. Kinkead has not fully understood the facts in the case," he wrote. According to the information John had gathered on his visit, Mahlo hadn't been fired, but simply "suspended for lack of funds."[491] "We are decidedly of the opinion that he had better be retained… . Mr. Mahlo's intercourse with Mr. Fred[k] Law Olmsted makes his services of decidedly greater value to the Board than would be those of an engineer who had not had equal opportunity of receiving ideas from Mr. Olmsted."[492]

A day later, John wrote to Kinkead. Apparently, Kinkead's preferred replacement for Mahlo had been a Col. Anderson.[493] John damned him with great praise—in an area other than landscape engineering. "I had a very pleasant conversation with Col. Anderson after you left me evening before last," he wrote to Kinkead. "I was much interested to find that he was an ardent civil service reformer. I suppose it is one of the beliefs of civil service reformers that no one should be turned out of office as long as he serves the public faithfully."[494]

That was where any semblance of placating Kinkead ended. John didn't even give Kinkead the respect of personally rebutting his facts or assertions. "As you were good enough to show Gen[l] Castleman the letter you wrote me he will doubtless in return acquaint you with the reasons I have given him for not favoring a change of engineer at this time," he told Kinkead. "His doing so will save me some trouble."[495]

The firm would have—and would need—John's forceful sense of certitude over the next twenty years as they continued to execute the projects Olmsted and Codman had laid out in Louisville and elsewhere.

In many ways, his talents at running a landscape architecture firm would exceed what Olmsted could have ever expected or hoped for. John would be a boon to the firm. And yet, in many ways, he would not be enough.

In the end, John would allow many things his father would not have. He would accommodate. He would do the job that was assigned to him. His father, though business savvy, had been at heart an artist carrying out his craft. John, though a man of some artistic sensibility, was a businessman doing a job.

In Louisville, the job changed. Influence on the Board of Park Commissioners shifted away from Cowan, now gone, towards Castleman. And whereas the original board president, Thomas Sherley, had seemed content as a figurehead—Castleman intended to use his office to influence the direction of the parks.

Eventually that direction would be back towards Castlewood, his 20-acre property east of town.

CHAPTER 15

CASTLEMAN RIDES AGAIN

In 1898, an American warship exploded near Spanish Cuba. What, exactly, had happened was unclear; it could have been a accidental magazine explosion.[496] But in the jingoistic climate of the day, it was enough. It meant war.[497]

The last time the United States had gone to war it was with the Confederate States. And John Breckinridge Castleman had been on the side that lost.

For the past two peaceable decades, Castleman had been the head of a Kentucky militia called The Louisville Legion. It was actually for this service—and not his Civil War days—that Castleman had been a "colonel."[498]

And so Colonel John Breckinridge Castleman volunteered his service to his country of second preference, and was commissioned an active colonel for the army of the United States. He mustered the Louisville Legion, First Regiment, and on August 6, 1898, the Legion arrived at the port town of Newport News, Virginia.

Colonel Castleman and his men did not go to Puerto Rico right away. Another gentleman-Colonel—Theodore Roosevelt—beat Castleman to the punch with his own band of volunteer "Rough Riders," and stormed San Juan Hill on his way to the presidency. The Navy was called to carry a garrison to Santiago, leaving Castleman in limbo. "You shall have a ship and a good one the moment we can get one to you," the reigning Adjutant General wrote to Castleman.[499]

After languishing a few more days in Virginia, Castleman and his men finally went to Puerto Rico.[500] Once there, Castleman took command of all the troops at Ponce. As a veteran member of many clubs, Castleman wasted no time in creating one. This one was called "The Patriotic Society of Porto Rico." The Society had three goals: 1) to instill "respect" for the government of the United States; 2) to demand "that no nude person of any age shall appear in any public place, street, or highway," which Castleman thought could be accomplished by legislation if persuasion was inadequate, and 3) "to encourage marriage everywhere in Porto Rico… among all people who live together as man and wife."[501] Whether these contributions turned the tide in the war effort remains an open question.

Castleman roamed the countryside with an entourage of eight non-coms and privates, capturing local rum and, briefly, imprisoning a Signal Corpsman for destroying shade trees on a public highway. As a Louisville park commissioner, Castleman had asked for more attention to the planting of the boulevard trees.[502] And here, he found "the destruction of trees on the Calle Real by the signal corps" to be "a piece of outrageous vandalism that can not be defended by any reason whatever."[503] He fumed that "growths of years and beauty and shade, giving necessary comfort to the whole public, have been destroyed."[504] Clearly, the colonel had not been a park commissioner for nothing.

This pro-tree bent may not have endeared him to all his troops. "Oh such warfare with a drunken man as commander and warring on inoffensive, ignorant nature workmen," one of his soldiers quipped.[505]

Of the 1,300 volunteers who set out, only 1,100 returned four months later. None of them saw combat. They simply went to Puerto Rico, drank the cheap and abundant local rum, contracted the abundant malaria and typhoid fever, and returned home reduced in number.[506]

On their way back, Castleman went to Washington, D.C., to persuade the Secretary of War to delay the regiment's triumphant return until Monday so a committee in Louisville could plan sufficiently for the welcome home.[507]

A few months later, when his service was essentially over, Castleman was made a Brigadier General, apparently by President McKinley himself.[508] And "General Castleman" is how he is known to this day.

In his memoirs many years later, General Castleman would go on for hundreds of pages about his plantation upbringing, his Civil War exploits, the peacetime command of the Louisville Legion, his non-combat Spanish War services.

And for his many years of service on the Board of Park Commissioners? Castleman wrote a page and a half.

CHAPTER 16

CASTLEMAN'S PARKS

The post-Olmsted years were years of adjustments, failures, and increasing deviations from the classic Frederick Law Olmsted principles. They were years of muddling execution rather than extraordinary vision. Which is to say they were important, but not always interesting.

But if John's work lacked the dazzle of his father's, the same could be said for the Park Commissioners in Louisville. Where his father had Cowan to work with, John had… Kinkead, Finzer, Castleman. In fact, John complained that Castleman had "practically usurped all power and there are various things going on that ought not to."[509]

So far, Kinkead had unsuccessfully proposed the zoo and the bird collection, which John had unceremoniously denied. In the coming years, Kinkead would propose other ideas that were anathema to the Olmsted ideals of park planning. Golf, for example. After learning, on one visit, about plans for a golf course in Cherokee Park, John wrote to Castleman: "The fear of being hit, or of having little children hit, would seriously detract from the pleasure of many people strolling in the park. No game where balls are propelled so swiftly ought to be allowed in a park so situated, so used, and so small as is Cherokee Park."[510] But the golf course would come to pass. In this new dynamic, Castleman and the Board were in the driver's seat—not the Olmsted firm.

Castleman had long been trying to get the Board of Park Commissioners to adopt Castlewood. Now, his time had come.

And John now had a chance to design a park all his own in Louisville, from start to finish. He was… somewhat less than thrilled with the project.

Tyler Park, named, after Mayor Henry Tyler, who had died in office in 1896, was built on two triangles of vacant land, which, according to John, "were of little value."[511] "On the upper side of the Avenue, 5 acres were acquired at a cost of $500 an acre," John recalled. On the lower side was Castlewood where "the General values his land at $2500 to $3000 an acre."[512] John thought that the cost, even at that 500-600 percent markup, was "not high." But Castleman was selling the land with the understanding that the Park Commission "should build and maintain a border road for lot frontage and this comes out of the area."[513] In other words, the Park Commission would be improving Castleman's property and raising its value.

The two triangles were divided by a massive stone bridge. Connecting the two halves of the park, going under the street, was a 40-foot arched tunnel that was originally intended for a street. John envisioned the park to consist of "a pleasant sloping lawn with ornamental shade trees," along side basketball courts, tennis courts, "etc."[514]

At the same time, the Olmsted firm was working on plans for Eastern Parkway on the western side of Castlewood. These would include a tree-lined median, the only section of any parkway in Louisville with such a feature. No doubt the parkway and Tyler Park served—and indeed continue to serve—to increase the values of the stately homes that now populate Castlewood.[515]

Castleman's will outlined how Castlewood was to be subdivided. The late general wanted big lots and big houses.[516] In 1903, he'd had Louisville's Park Engineer, Cecil Fraser, draw up plans to that effect. "Castlewood is unique," gushed the development's promotional text. "There is no part of beautiful "Cherokee Park" so beautiful."[517]

CHAPTER 17

LOUISVILLE: CITY OF PARKS

If you live in Miami, you go to the beach. If you live in Denver, you go to the mountains. In Louisville, you go to the parks.

Even in their early years, the parks were a massive success.

At 676 acres, Iroquois Park "is one of the finest in the country," wrote the *Courier-Journal* in 1917, "as it offers not only beautiful drives for all sorts of vehicles, but pleasant walks for pedestrians. From its highest point the view is superb. The city as well as the country adjacent to it offer a picture that must be seen to be fully appreciated."[518]

Cherokee Park's 409 acres, the paper said, contain "scenery that is difficult to match. Superb and umbrageous trees, standing singly and in groups, are to be seen there in higher perfection than in almost any other park in the country. Stately maples, lofty poplars, great oaks, giant sycamores, graceful elms, and black walnuts are plentiful in this park… Through it flows the middle fork of Beargrass Creek, adding to the majestic beauty of the grounds."[519]

As for Shawnee, "it seems to have been designed to become the meeting place for thousands of lovers of athletic sports and games"—which surely had not been Olmsted's chief intention for the now 181 acres along the Ohio River—"and from early spring to late in the fall wildest use is made of the baseball diamonds and tennis courts."[520] Shawnee had boaters and swimmers and grazing sheep and a bandstand flanked by 10,000 pansies as the sun set over the Indiana hills.[521]

Of course, there was also Tyler Park. The paper credited Castleman with donating his land for Tyler Park, which of course he didn't, having sold the land at a considerable mark-up to the public. "Adjacent to Castlewood," the paper described it, which of course it was, and for less-than-altruistic reasons.[522] But even Tyler Park was a hit and reportedly attracted a crowd of 10,000 in for a Fourth of July festival.[523]

There was an amusement park next to Shawnee called Riverview Park. In 1907, it became the site of White City Louisville, a knock-off replica of Olmsted's Chicago Court of Honor, complete with white facades and a central lagoon.

They needn't have bothered. Louisville didn't need a replica of Olmsted's work. With three large parks and an extensive system of parkways, the city now boasted one of the most comprehensive Olmsted park systems in the country. The White City closed after just two years.[524]

In 1902, in another callback to the World's Colombian Exposition, a reported fifty thousand people endured a pouring rain in Cherokee Park. While a band played "Dixie," and when they stopped, the granddaughter of art patron C.C. Bickel, pulled a ribbon, parting the fabric to reveal Enid Yandell's Daniel Boone, now cast in bronze and raised on a stone pedestal. John Breckinridge Castleman spoke and denounced socialism and social unrest and "the influence of demagoguery." "And so today," he said, "we come together that we may pay tribute to a splendid example of vital citizenship." Pioneers such as Boone, "have largely completed the tasks that they were called to do," Castleman said.[525] And so had he.

In Castleman's twilight years, a committee of his friends commissioned a bronze statute of him riding a horse, to be erected in the middle of a traffic circle at the intersection of Cherokee Road and Cherokee Parkway.[526]

And so was immortalized the horse ride that was already, in Castleman's own estimation, one of the great marvels of the Chicago World's Fair some twenty years prior.[527]

Apparently, a large crowd assembled for the unveiling on November 8,

1913. The Mayor and the Lieutenant Governor were both present. The Superintendent allowed local teachers and schoolchildren to attend. The drum and bugle corps of the Kentucky National Guard played the music.

Castleman finally retired from the Board of Park Commissioners at age 76. In his farewell report, Castleman wrote, "Louisville has a park system that is not equaled by any park system in the world… . Nowhere can be found more beauty or more attractions than here."[528]

Indeed, thanks to the work of Cowan and Olmsted and John and even Castleman, Louisville became a city of parks. Where Central Park in Manhattan and Prospect Park in Brooklyn total 1,428 acres to serve a combined 4.2 million people in those two boroughs,[529] Louisville's three large Frederick Law Olmsted parks total 1,398 acres to serve just 760,000 people.[530] In addition to many recreational parks, Louisville also has a 6,500-acre woodland in the southwest called Jefferson Memorial Forest.[531] And even now, 4,000 acres of new park lands are opening on the city's eastern edge. These are conscientious descendants of Iroquois, Shawnee, and Cherokee.[532]

It has become impossible to separate Louisville from the parks Olmsted and his firm designed for it. The city is Olmsted's living legacy—one of many.

CHAPTER 18

TURNING BACK THE CLOCK

Sometimes history goes backwards.

Exactly one week after the Castleman statue was dedicated near Cherokee Park, the *Courier-Journal* ran a full-length story under the headline [533]

SEGREGATION OF RACES URGED

The paper's own chief mechanic, W.D. Binford, had advocated for racial segregation in an address to the Louisville Real Estate Exchange, and this, somehow, was enough for the paper to run a full article on his belief that Louisville should pass a housing segregation ordinance, as Baltimore had in 1911.[534]

The law Binford cited would make it illegal for white people to rent or own buildings "in any colored block," or for African-Americans to live in white blocks, except as servants. In Baltimore, Binford said, "the colored element… invaded the white districts and purchased property wherever it was offered for sale."[535] While buying a house that is for sale might seem like an entirely benign exercise of one's legal rights, to Binford, "this naturally engendered bad feeling between the races, and riots in many sections of Baltimore followed. This we hope to avoid by prompt action here."[536]

In fact, this was but the latest example of a racist revival spreading across the South, and even across some border states such as Kentucky and Maryland.

Beginning with the 1896 *Plessy v. Ferguson* decision of the U.S. Supreme Court, which enshrined "separate but equal" and state-sponsored apartheid, there had been a growing boldness in the effort to keep black people away from white people in public spaces.[537]

Lynchings were commonplace in the South around the beginning of the 20th century. There had been a lynching in Maysville, Kentucky—about 150 miles from Louisville—in 1899. The *Courier-Journal* ran a highly critical letter to the editor, which lamented, "no more cruel, brutal, barbarous, devilish deed ever marked the records of savages."[538] Five years later, there was a lynching in Russellville, near Bowling Green.[539]

It was an environment ripe for terror, oppression, fear. Since its re-birth in 1915, the Ku Klux Klan had become a social and political force across the country by appealing to blatant racism, as well as the discomfort of rural white men with the country's shift from rural to urban life.[540] The Klan made several attempts to organize a Louisville branch. In August 1921, the Klan placed an ad in Louisville newspapers seeking recruits. Mayor George Weissinger Smith took them on. "In the disguise of a law supporter, [the Klan] countenances crimes as horrible as those it seeks to punish," the mayor said. "I shall use every lawful means to prevent and suppress its growth in our community. As long as I am Mayor, there will be no Kuklux Klan in Louisville."[541] A month later, at the mayor's request, the Louisville Board of Public Safety denied the Klan permission to rent a theater.[542] And yet…

The city had already given in to this climate of hatred. First, with the housing ordinance, which the Supreme Court overturned in 1917, and then with the parks.[543] Yes, Louisville segregated the parks.

As early as 1914, the Board of Park Commissioners had segregated the tennis courts, reasoning that "*some provision* for negroes in Shawnee, Iroquois and Cherokee Parks," should be made (italics mine).[544] Even that concession to separate "equality" was controversial. At least some whites wanted to keep African-Americans out of the parks altogether.[545]

Castleman agreed. Showing his Confederate colors once again, he extended the tennis court segregation the *entire* park—all of the parks. He asserted in a *Courier-Journal* op-ed that "We have inexcusably neglected to provide recreation grounds for our negro fellow citizens," as if all the parks hitherto built suddenly did not apply to African-Americans. "These people are citizens," the general allowed, in magnanimous condescension. "The same right that induces our liberal provision for their separate education should impel us to provide for them separate recreation grounds."[546]

So, in order to maintain "separate but equal," they would build separate, "Negro" parks for the black Louisvillians to use. Right at the same time that Mayor Smith was trying to keep the Ku Klux Klan from meeting in Louisville, construction was underway on a new park, designed by what was left of the Olmsted firm, and situated just a few blocks south of Shawnee. Chickasaw Park opened in 1922 as a 61-acre consolation prize, "provided for the use of negroes."[547]

The parks Olmsted and Cowan had worked so hard to bring to life, and which they had meant from inception to be open for all people, were fully segregated in 1924. By then, Frederick Law Olmsted had been long gone, and Andrew Cowan, John Olmsted, and even John Castleman were all dead.

CHAPTER 19

LEGACY

From 1907-1908, Andrew Cowan did a second tour on the Park Commission, and for a short time, he even served as president.[548] This tenure was much less eventful, though he did work on Shelby Park, which became the centerpiece of a beautiful working class neighborhood near downtown.

Then he built a big Tudor mansion, perched on a hill overlooking the Beargrass valley and the eastern most edge of Cherokee Park. His backyard ran down to the creek, in a place where mallards sheltered their ducklings on the banks and courted in the calm waters. He had the Olmsted firm design the grounds.[549]

Andrew Cowan died in 1919.[550] He was buried in Cave Hill Cemetery—the Cherokee Park of cemeteries. His coffin was draped with the flag of the United States and the Greek Cross emblem of his artillery brigade of the Sixth Army of the Potomac. Taps sounded on the bugle.[551]

As John Breckinridge Castleman had once written, "No one [did] more in the early days of the board than he."[552] This is undoubtedly true. But few remember Cowan now. No statue burnishes the glory of Andrew Cowan; no park system bears his name.

Castleman retired to spend his last years in Eau Gallie, Florida. He sent oranges—still exotic—back to his friends in Louisville.[553] When he died in 1918,[554] his land went to his wife, Alice.[555] It became a subdivision of beautiful mansions in the Tyler Park Neighborhood.

On a pedestal near Cherokee Park, he still rides on his mare from the Chicago World's Fair, a genteel general in bronze.

John C. Olmsted died in 1920.[556] He had his share of professional success, but after toiling so long in the shadow of Frederick Law Olmsted, he was later eclipsed by Frederick Law Olmsted, Jr.[557]

In 1899, Rick established the American Society of Landscape Architects. Two years later, barely in his thirties, he was appointed a professor of landscape architecture at Harvard.[558] Rick became the nearest his generation had to his father—leading a firm that designed the National Mall and Rock Creek Park in Washington, DC, as well as Bernheim Forest near Louisville. He achieved the success his father had wanted for him all along.[559]

Ever since they were built, the parks have faced threats—some of them existential. There were the 30 years of segregation (the parks were legally re-integrated in the 1950s).[560] There was an international airport built near Iroquois Park. A sewage overflow system was put through Beargrass Creek, dumping raw effluent when it rains. An interstate highway was also put through Cherokee Park, but public opposition force transportation officials to tunnel under a hill on the north side. There were tornadoes in 1974, which ripped out many of the original trees of Cherokee Park and laid their hulls to rot on the hillsides.

Some of the wrongs, such as segregation, have been righted; others, such as the sewage, have simply been endured.

But the parks are resilient. They are lovely scenery. And if you go to the parks today, you can still forget you are in the middle of a city.

There will be a gate, then some trees, then a field, then some trees, and then…

Epilogue

Early in the day, when we had mostly gotten snow and sleet and it was still safe to walk outside, I went on one of my habitual walks to Cherokee Park—at the time, a necessity to help me escape the stress of law school. Ice had accumulated in floats on the surface of Beargrass Creek and formed in sheets with the curves of an aurora borealis—blue, white, and grey—glacial ice, marbled on the water.

I climbed a ridge above the creek, turning my feet sideways, like a clown, to keep traction in the inches of sleet. When I got to the top, I saw a broad, big hill, wooded and snow-covered, separated from me by a deep valley. For a moment I was lost. In all my wanderings in the Park, I thought, I had never seen that place. I must be somewhere else, somewhere new. My heart leapt at the possibility for getting lost in the woods in the city is a privilege. And then I saw the tennis courts and knew where I was.

As I stood there recovering my bearings, a bird flew in front of me and landed on a tree branch not twenty feet to my left. It was small and rusty-brown, with a rusty-cream breast and a white stripe over the eyes. I thought it looked like a chipmunk, so I remembered it as "the chipmunk bird." It hopped around the branches and sang. I thought of its song as "happy," in the same way that a novice wine drinker thinks, "This wine tastes 'good.'"

Over the course of the day and into the night, the freezing rain fell and the trees turned to glass. The ice storm would remembered mostly for the havoc it wrought. But I also remembered it as the day I started paying attention to the birds in my surroundings. What I discovered when I did was a vast, colorful, and somewhat parallel universe.

Cherokee Park was at the center of it.

Major Waltman of the Louisville Olmsted Parks Conservancy stooped down to get a feather off the grass. (Unlike the Civil War veterans who led to the park's creation, "Major" is his name, not his title.)

"What kind of feather is that, that you just picked up?" I asked him.

"Um," he considered, "it looks like a great-horned owl feather."

"*Really,*" I said, surprised.

"Yeah. There's a pair of great-horned owls that has lived in this park for probably twenty years or more."

"*Really.*"

"May not be the same two birds, but it's a pair."

The Olmsted Parks Conservancy is a non-profit organization that arose in response to the 1974 tornadoes that obliterated much of Cherokee Park.[569]

"There's an *extremely* diverse bird population in the park," Waltman continued. "We get a tremendous number of migrating warbler species through here during the spring and fall migration. So the birds are using this as a stopover for feeding so they can go to the next stage."

An airplane whizzed overhead.

"Then we have a fair number of resident birds that nest here, probably in the neighborhood of sixty, seventy (species)..."

The grass crunched underfoot as we marched.

"I'm hearing one in particular," he told me. "It's a yellow-throated warbler that nests here, you'll hear him in a minute, he'll go teu-teu-teu-teu-teu," Major said, in a descending rough approximation of the birdsong.

We stopped and waited a few seconds. Nothing.

"He'll make a liar out of me," Major muttered, throwing a twig onto the grass.

Then, sure enough, we heard it. A sweet, ethereal chiming, going ever more quickly down the scale. *Teu-teu-teu-teu.* "Huh," I said. "Yellow-throated warbler."

After the ice storm, I got a bird book and started learning names. When I went outside, I'd listen for the songs, then try to remember them until I got home so I could look them up.

I began thinking of birds mnemonically. The "chipmunk bird" was actually a Carolina wren. It's a small bird with a big voice. The "happy song" I heard is often rendered as *tea-kettle, tea-kettle, tea-kettle!* but I remembered it as a rapid-fire *figaro-figaro-figaro!*—if you're near one, it's as easy to miss as Plácido Domingo belting out Rossini's famous aria from a comparable distance. Cardinals became "the laser-gun birds" or "the sprinkler birds" because they sing variations of *tck tck tck piu piu piu*. Mockingbirds were "the car-alarm birds" because they cycle through several different song bits before starting over again (*piu piu piu, ooee ooee ooee, ticktock ticktock ticktock,* etc.). Pileated woodpeckers were the "jungle-monkey birds" or "the dolphin birds." Starlings were "the robot birds," for their weird assortment of clicks and squeals and rattles.

Birds do sing in winter, though not as often as they do in spring (what we hear as birdsong is essentially the bird saying "*This land is my land; no trespassing,*" or "*Mate with me, mate with me, mate with me PLEASE!*"). But the bleakness of the winter landscape can make birds stand out all the more, both sonically and visually, and this may be why I noticed the Carolina wren, when I had never really paid attention to birds before.

Often, it's easier to hear a bird and then try to spot it. The first time I did this I was walking to the Park on a crisp morning, and I heard a cheerful and melancholy *see-bee see-bay*. Carolina chickadees are small birds (and pretty, with a distinctive black-and-white head), and it took me a while to find it. When I did, I was amazed, both by the smallness of the bird and the beauty of its song.

One of my favorite birdsongs quickly became a slurry whistle that started high and dropped low across three different pitches, very nearly in musical thirds. The third note tended to bounce along a few times. Sometimes it started lower and went up the scale. The song could be quite clear and go for a distance. I could even hear it inside, through walls and windows. In my own rendering, I thought it sounded like *peeee-aaa-weee da dee da dee da dee*, so I thought the bird was an Eastern pewee (I am from a town called Pewee Valley).

But I never could spot the bird when it was singing. I knew what I was looking for—a small gray songbird. I could listen to two of the birds calling back and forth for fifteen minutes. Sometimes I would join in the whistling (which I don't think they noticed). Once I saw one at the top of a telephone pole but it was too far away to see well; once I saw one in a holly tree but from below, so I couldn't see anything definitive. I never saw the bird well enough to confirm that it was a pewee.

Then, I got a monocular (it's like binoculars with only one eyepiece; I call it "the scope"). Like a nearsighted person putting on glasses for the first time, my world suddenly expanded. Birds I'd often dismissed as common sparrows or robins became numerous in their diversity—finches and wrens and waxwings and warblers.

Later that spring, I heard the pewee song in Cherokee Park, in a strip of brush near one of the tree borders. I tracked it down, and through the lens of my scope at long last I saw my quarry—and it wasn't a pewee at all. In its place was a brown bird, a little bigger than a finch, with white flecks on its body and yellow, white, and black on its face.

It was like getting lost in the Park. I consulted my bird book. It looked like a few of them, but none were definitive (though if I'd noticed the white circle below the beak, that would have sealed it). I decided to call Major Waltman. Getting his voicemail, I explained the situation and did my best imitation of the birdsong. Because of a phone glitch, I wouldn't get Major's reply for another few months, when I ran into him in the Park. He remembered my message, and when I whistled the tune again, he finally confirmed what the mystery bird was: a white-throated sparrow. Bird books have the song as *old man Peabody Peabody Peabody*.

As I learned their songs and characteristics, the presence of the birds became a great comfort to me. I could step out my door and hear a song that was beautiful and familiar. Birds became friends on my walks, spirits in the woods. I shamelessly anthropomorphized them, ascribing personalities based on their patterns of behavior. I imagined the songbirds saying hello, and the blue jays and starlings as the bullies of the neighborhood, and birds of prey— hawks and owls—as majestic overlords of the forest.

One day, along Beargrass Creek, I glimpsed a big-beaked, blue-green bird sitting on a branch. I knew it was a belted kingfisher, though I'd seen one only in pictures. I looked through the scope and saw him in all his regality (he's got head-feathers that poof up to make a kind of crown) for the briefest moment before he took off. I took off after him, running along the edge of the creek. His rattling song—a battle cry that must strike fear into the hearts of fish and frogs—trailed off as he got further away. I stopped, heart pounding, to see if he'd landed on a new branch. I looked around, trying to suppress my nerves. Then I spotted him and raised my scope. And he took off again.

This began a series of such encounters with the kingfisher. For me, he's the most spectral of birds, a phantom always in motion, never still long enough for you to get him, even by sight. Sometimes I only hear his rattle as he flies by. Even that gets my blood going.

Birds are generous in their mysteries and surprises. If I go out looking for a specific unusual bird (say, a scarlet tanager), I almost never find it. But when I'm not looking, something astonishing presents itself to me.

Birding is a form of meditation—it is all about listening, awareness, openness to whatever comes your way. You must pay attention to the moment *right now*. There is nothing else; there is only this. And then, like a kingfisher, it is gone.

Two days after I first saw the kingfisher, I spotted a red-shouldered hawk eating a mole. Hawks are easier. You can almost follow them from tree to tree. They fly with much grace and little sound. Sometimes you hear them screech, and sometimes you only hear blue jays imitating them. Once, a hawk swooped up right in front of me.

I've seen a great-horned owl and great blue herons resting on their perches, as imperturbable as old men asleep in their chairs. I've seen hummingbirds drinking from orange trumpet-shaped flowers. I've been enveloped by the ethereal high-pitched purring of cedar waxwings. I've seen northern-flickers shadow-boxing on a branch, their long beaks in the air, saffron-tinged tails fanned out, each waiting for the right time to make his move in a high stakes battle for mating rights and territory. I've been cheered on days both sunny and dreary by the trillings of song sparrows, the tea-drinking of towhees and the happy babblings of house finches. I've watched indigo buntings—the lapis lazuli of birds, like they were painted by Vermeer—chase each other in meadows of wildflowers.

I began to dream of birds, just as I sometimes dream in Spanish. I dreamt of birds I had never seen and would never see, rare birds, resplendent birds that I had a tough time identifying, birds I knew shouldn't be there. Sometimes I could just make them out.

And then sometimes I go to the Park and walk through the same dream.

Through the gate without a gate. Into the shade of the beeches, their elephantine bark rising sixty feet and branching into delicate strokes. This is an in-between world—where you can look at the faces of the mansions on the other side of the road and at the same time be startled by the guttural call of a barred owl.

Deeper into the woods, you go, until with another step you leave the woods and pass into a meadow. The temperature drops. The city can still be heard, but it cannot be seen. In a matter of minutes, all of the busyness of modern life—the commerce, the traffic—peel away.

You hear the song of a woodthrush. And really, you have never heard anything so lovely in your entire life as the song of a woodthrush in the dark woods. It is the Elvish of birdsong—slow and leisurely and ethereal and all-enveloping—like a fairy tossing gold coins down through the leaves.

You are now in the Park. And if you pay attention, what you are seeing will never be happen again. There is only this moment. And this moment. And this moment.

Walk across a meadow, where sheep used to graze, surrounded by birdsong, past a couple lying on a blanket on the grass, or a group of children playing kickball, or a family reunion, or a pair of runners who've just made it up the hill.

This is the best of Birkenhead Park transmuted. Olmsted has imported one of his favorite places. And improved it.

Go down the sloped path. Soon you can see the creek. If it hasn't rained recently, the creek will crawl by, at the bottom of a ditch of its own making. If it has rained, it will tear the soil away from its banks, carry trees and tires, dam itself on the supports of its bridges.

There's a path going straight down the hill. You can only scramble down the dirt by catching rock holds and roots. But when you get to the bottom, you are at the creek. Bathing robins scatter to the nearby trees.

Find the place where the creek hits an island. As it bends around the island, the creek becomes a gurgling brook.

The music of water has tone but no melody, many rhythms instead of one, each moment a sound going into the next and the next and the next…

Stand there under the gaze of goldfinches and let your mind drift with the current.

Acknowledgments

I owe thanks to a great many people for helping with this book. To Gill Holland first and foremost—as with so many things in Louisville, this began as an idea of his. To Rebecca Summer, who wrote a fantastic undergraduate thesis at Yale that provided the spark for this project—especially the Confederate and segregation elements of the story. This book owes an awful lot to three predecessors: Witold Rybczynski's biography of Frederick Law Olmsted, *A Clearing in the Distance*; Erik Larson's *The Devil in the White City*, and *Origins of the Olmsted Parks & Parkways* by Louisville's own, the late Samuel Thomas. Thanks also to the staff in the Manuscript Reading Room at the Library of Congress; Bruce Allar for his wisdom; Dan Crutcher for allowing me to use pieces of stories I'd previously written on aspects of the park for *Louisville Magazine*; Josh Moss for good, writerly feedback; Heather Backus for great, wonderful guidance; Siri Setzer for the Dickens reference; Jim Holmberg and the rest of the Filson Historical Society staff for research assistance; Temple Bodley for writing a damn good kernel of this story almost 100 years ago; Mimi Zinniel and the good people at the Olmsted Parks Conservancy for providing resources on long-term loan, and for helping maintain the Olmsted parks and parkways Louisville is so lucky to have; Sean, Missy, and Matt for being the best staff at Safai, the best coffee shop in Louisville; Hound Dog Press and Mike Kennedy for kick ass layout and design; Stephanie Kertis for shepherding this project to the shelves.

To my wife, Brooke, thank you for everything.

NOTES

Abbreviations

FLO = Frederick Law Olmsted
JCO = John Charles Olmsted
FLO, Jr. = Frederick Law Olmsted, Jr. also known as "Rick"
JBC = John Breckinridge Castleman
LOC = Library of Congress

Manuscript Sources

Collections

Olmsted Parks Conservancy, Louisville, KY
- Beveridge, Charles and Levee, Arleyn, "Louisville's Olmsted Park Legacy: Cherokee, Iroquois and Shawnee Parks and the Parkways" (draft), 1992
- Beveridge, Charles and Levee, Arleyn, "Olmsted Documentary Resource for Louisville's Park Legacy: Cherokee, Iroquois, and Shawnee Parks and the Parkways," 1992
- Levee, Arleyn, ed., Louisville's Olmsted Park Legacy: Selective Chronology, 1992
- Richardson, Artemas and Hudak, Joseph, eds., Journal of the Development of Cherokee Park, 1891-1974, (commissioned by Olmsted Associates, Inc. 1974, available at the Olmsted Parks Conservancy)

ProQuest Historical Newspapers, available online courtesy of the Louisville Free Public Library
- Courier-Journal
- Daily Courier
- Louisville Daily Journal
- The Louisville Times

The Library of Congress, Manuscript Division, Washington, DC
- Frederick Law Olmsted Archive
- Olmsted Associates Archive

The Filson Historical Society, Louisville, KY
- Papers of Young Allison
- Papers of William R. Belknap
- Papers of Temple Bodley
- Filson Club History Quarterly, Kent Masterson Brown, Vol. 59 (Filson Historical Society, July 1985)
- Papers of Andrew Cowan
- Papers of R.T. Durrett
- Papers of Thomas Henry Hines
- Papers of William Onderdonk
- Official Minutes of the Board of Park Commissioners, Louisville Parks & Recreation Collection
- Papers of Enid Yandell

University of Louisville Photographic Archives online

Other Contemporary Sources
- Castleman, John Breckinridge. Active Service (Courier-Journal Job Printing Co 1917)
- Dickens, Charles. Bleak House (Bantam Books 1853)
- Dickens, Charles. American Notes for General Circulation. (Penguin Classics 1989)
- Johnston, J. Stoddard, ed. Memorial History of Louisville (American Biographical Publishing Co. 1896)
- Olmsted, Frederick Law and Sutton, S.B., ed. Civilizing American Cities: Writings on Landscapes (De Capo Press 1997)
- Twombly, Robert, ed. Frederick Law Olmsted: Essential Texts, Robert Twombly, ed, (W.W. Norton & Company 2010)

Modern Sources
- Berger, John. Forests Forever (University of Chicago Press 2008)
- Catton, Bruce. Bruce Catton's Civil War: Three Volumes in One (The Fairfax Press 1984)
- Crowe-Carraco, Carol. Women Who Made a Difference. (University Press of Kentucky 1989)
- Freese, Barbara. Coal: A Human History by (Perseus Books 2003)
- Goodwin, Doris Kearns. Team of Rivals (Simon & Schuster 2005)
- Kleber, John, ed. The Kentucky Encyclopedia, (University Press of Kentucky 1992)
- Peterson, Jon. The Birth of City Planning in the United States, 1840-1917 (Johns Hopkins University Press 2003)
- Kleberp, John, ed. Encyclopedia of Louisville (University Press of Kentucky 2001)
- McPherson, James. Battle Cry of Freedom (Oxford University Press 1988)
- Martin, Justin. Genius of Place (Da Capo 2011)
- Mann, Charles. 1491: New Revelations of the Americas before Columbus (Vintage Books 2006)

Larson, Erik. The Devil in the White City, Erik Larson (Vintage Books 2004)

New York City Government, "List of Parks by Total Acreage," NYC.gov, www1.nyc.gov/assets/buildings/excel/dpr_park_list.xls

Klotter, James. Kentucky: Portrait in Paradox, 1900-1950 (Kentucky Historical Society 1996)

Public Broadcasting System, The American Experience, "The Ku Klux Klan in the 1920s," pbs.org/wgbh/americanexperience/features/general-article/flood-klan

Soans, Catherine and Stevenson, Agnus, eds. Concise Oxford English Dictionary (Oxford University Press 2006)

Summer, Rebecca. "Partnership for a Democratic Society: Frederick Law Olmsted, Andrew Cowan, and the Louisville Park System," Yale University Thesis 2010.

Rybczysnki, Witold. A Clearing in the Distance (Scribner 2000)

Thomas, Samuel. Origins of Louisville's Olmsted Parks and Parkways (Holland Brown Books 2013)

U.S. Census Bureau

West Egg Inflation Calculator, westegg.com/inflation/

Endnotes

1.   Twombly, Robert, ed, *Frederick Law Olmsted Essential Texts* (W.W. Norton & Company 2010), p. 42.
2.   Twombly, *Essential Texts*, p. 42.
3.   Twombly, *Essential Texts*, p. 42.
4.   Twombly, *Essential Texts*, p. 42.
5.   Twombly, *Essential Texts*, p. 42.
6.   Twombly, *Essential Texts*, p. 42.
7.   Twombly, *Essential Texts*, p. 42.
8.   Rybczynski, Witold, *A Clearing in the Distance* (Scribner 2000), p. 34.
9.   Twombly, *Essential Texts*, pp. 43-44.
10.   Twombly, *Essential Texts*, p. 319.
11.   "Embellishment of Grounds," *Louisville Daily Courier*, Apr. 8, 1854.
12.   Charles Dickens, *Bleak House* (Bantam Books 1853) p. 1.
13.   "A Terrible Accident," *Courier-Journal*, Sep 23, 1883 (ProQuest Historical Newspapers)
14.   "Down in a Coal Mine," *Courier-Journal*, Feb 13, 1884 (ProQuest Historical Newspapers)
15.   "Death in a Coal Mine," *Courier-Journal*, Aug 12, 1885 (ProQuest Historical Newspapers)
16.   Freese, Barbara. *Coal: A Human History* by Barbara Freese (Perseus Books 2003) p. 175
17.   "Coal at Louisville," *Courier-Journal*, May 13, 1880 (ProQuest Historical Newspapers) pg. 3.
18.   "Down in a Coal Mine," *Courier-Journal*, May 12, 1887 (ProQuest Historical Newspapers pg. 6)
19.   "A Terrible Accident," *Courier-Journal*, Jun 18, 1886 (ProQuest Historical Newspapers)
20.   "Run Over by a Coal Cart," *Courier-Journal*, Sep 26, 1883 (ProQuest Historical Newspapers)
21.   "Cheap Coal," *Courier-Journal*, Apr 26, 1882 (ProQuest Historical Newspapers)
22.   Freese, *Coal*, p. 148.
23.   Freese, *Coal*, pp. 83-84, 153.
24.   Freese, *Coal*, p. 153
25.   "After Fresh Air," *Courier-Journal*, July 17, 1885 (ProQuest Historical Newspapers). There was a prevalent theory at the time that air could be "foul" as if it had spoiled like milk and that this bad air was responsible for a host of illnesses. While misguided in the particulars, this theory was correct in many of its prognoses. See, Freese, *Coal*, p. 146.
26.   "Fresh-Air Excursion," *Courier-Journal*, August 7, 1881 (ProQuest Historical Newspapers) p. 6.
27.   "After Fresh Air," *Courier-Journal*, July 17, 1885 (ProQuest Historical Newspapers) p. 6
28.   "Orphan's Day," *Courier-Journal*, July 24, 1881 (ProQuest Historical Newspapers) p. 8
29.   "Orphan's Day," *Courier-Journal*, July 24, 1881, p. 8.
30.   "Orphan's Day," *Courier-Journal*, July 24, 1881, p. 8.
31.   "The Epidemic of 1878," *Courier-Journal*, Sep 23, 1888 (ProQuest Historical Newspapers)
32.   "Typhoid Fever," *Courier-Journal*, Nov 16, 1881 (ProQuest Historical Newspapers)
33.   "The Week's Dead," *Courier-Journal*, Aug 26, 1883 (ProQuest Historical Newspapers)
34.   Peterson, Jon. *The Birth of City Planning in the United States*, 1840-1917, p 30
35.   "The Cholera: Seventy-three Deaths in Nashville Yesterday…" *Courier-Journal*, Jun 21, 1873 (ProQuest Historical Newspapers); "The Cholera: Louisville's Past Experience With the Dread Disease…" *Courier-Journal*, Jul 3, 1885 (ProQuest Historical Newspapers)
36.   Peterson, *Birth of City Planning*, p 30.
37.   "The Doctors and the Cholera," *Courier-Journal*, Aug 5, 1883 (ProQuest Historical Newspapers)
38.   Peterson, *Birth of City Planning*, p 14.
39.   Kearns Goodwin, Doris. *Team of Rivals* (Simon & Schuster 2005) pp. 418-419.
40.   Dickens, Charles. *American Notes for General Circulation* (Penguin Classics 1989) p. 212. Louisville Encyclopedia, pp. 327, 716.
41.   Speed, James. "Engineer's Department," *Daily Courier*, May 11, 1854 (ProQuest Historical Newspapers)
42.   "Report of the Health Officer to the Board of Health," *Louisville Daily Journal*, Jun 14, 1866 (ProQuest Historical Newspapers).
43.   Kleberp, John. ed. *Encyclopedia of Louisville*, (University Press of Kentucky 2001) p. 514; "Table 11. Population of the 100 Largest Urban Places: 1880," U.S. Bureau of the Census, http://www.census.gov/population/www/documentation/twps0027/tab11.txt (accessed 11/9/2013)
44.   Peterson, *Birth of City Planning*, pp. 30-33.
45.   Peterson, *Birth of City Planning*, pp. 30-33.
46.   Peterson, *Birth of City Planning*, p. 36
47.   Peterson, *Birth of City Planning*, p. 36
48.   Peterson, *Birth of City Planning*, p. 40
49.   Peterson, *Birth of City Planning*, pp. 30-33.

50. Peterson, *Birth of City Planning*, p. 42
51. "Louisville waterworks: The Water to be Turned on To-Day," *Daily Courier*, Oct 15, 1860 (ProQuest Historical Newspapers)
52. "The City Sewers," *Daily Courier*, Oct 24, 1868 (ProQuest Historical Newspapers)
53. "A Look from the Highland Suburb of Louisville," *Courier-Journal*, Jun 16, 1872 (ProQuest Historical Newspapers)
54. Thomas, *Origins*, p. 105.
55. Thomas, *Origins*, pp. 59-64.
56. Thomas, *Origins*, pp. 36-38.
57. Thomas, *Origins*, p. 36
58. Thomas, *Origins*, p. 38
59. Brown, Kent Masterson. "Double Canister at Ten Yards: Captain Andrew Cowan at Gettysburg," T*he Filson Club History Quarterly*, Vol. 59, July 1985, p. 293.
60. Letter from Augustus Wilson to Temple Bodley, Apr. 13, 1929, Filson Historical Society
61. Brown, "Double Canister at Ten Yards," p. 293.
62. Brown, "Double Canister at Ten Yards," p. 293.
63. "Captain Andrew Cowan's 1st New York Independent Battery Light Artillery within Confederate works on the Petersburg line," Library of Congress, Call number LC-B811- 2343[P&P]. It's impossible to tell from the distance at which the photograph was taken whether this person was actually Cowan or was simply one of Cowan's men, but the point remains that it was Cowan's battery. For Siege of Petersburg, see McPherson, James. *Battle Cry of Freedom* (Oxford University Press 1988) pp. 778-780. General Ulysses Grant had instructed his soldiers to turn "the Shenandoah Valley [into] a barren waste… so that cros flying over it for the balance of this season will have to carry their provender with them." This they did.
64. Brown, "Double Canister at Ten Yards," p. 293.
65. Encyclopedia of Louisville, p. 228.
66. Cowan, Andrew. "The Public Parks and Parkways," Andrew Cowan, Memorial History of Louisville from Its First Settlement to the Year 1896, edited by J. Stoddard Johnston, (American Biographical Publishing Co. 1896) p. 338.
67. "The Public Parks and Parkways," Andrew Cowan, Memorial History of Louisville from Its First Settlement to the Year 1896, edited by J. Stoddard Johnston, (American Biographical Publishing Co. 1896) p. 338.
68. *Memorial History of Louisville*, p. 338.
69. Berger, John. *Forests Forever* (University of Chicago Press 2008) p. 35.
70. Berger, *Forests Forever*, p. 34
71. Rybczynski, *Clearing in the Distance*, p. 34.
72. Rybczynski, *Clearing in the Distance*, pp. 23-24.
73. Rybczynski, *Clearing in the Distance*, pp. 24-25.
74. Rybczynski, *Clearing in the Distance*, pp. 25-26, 29.
75. Rybczynski, *Clearing in the Distance*, p. 45.
76. Martin, Justin. Genius of Place (Da Capo 2011) pp. 17-18; Rybczynski, *Clearing in the Distance*, pp. 36-37. Actually, Rybczynski speculates that Olmsted actually had vernal keratoconjunctivitis, a spring-based ocular disease which occurs in late childhood or early adulthood. Rybczynski also suspects that Olmsted simply didn't want to do the necessary cramming necessary to gain admission to college. Nevertheless, Olmsted understood his plight as having been sparked by the sumac poisoning. And it is that understanding which would have shaped his own perceptions, choices, and still-forming identity.
77. Rybczynski, *Clearing in the Distance*, pp. 39-40.
78. Rybczynski, *Clearing in the Distance*, pp. 42-46.
79. Rybczynski, *Clearing in the Distance*, pp. 54-58.
80. Rybczynski, *Clearing in the Distance*, pp. 58-59.
81. Martin, *Genius of Place*, pp. 40-41.
82. Martin, *Genius of Place*, pp. 40-41; Rybczynski, *Clearing in the Distance*, pp. 63.
83. Martin, *Genius of Place*, pp. 159-160.
84. Rybczinski, *Clearing in the Distance*, pp. 376, 423-424; Larson, *The Devil in the White City*, pp. 51, 53.
85. Belknap, William, "Some Notes on 'Salmagundi,'" Papers of W. R. Belknap (Filson Historical Society, undated but the last date referenced in the text is February 6, 1890).pp. 3-4. Belknap had suggested the name, which he'd used for a discussion section in a magazine he edited at Princeton, having stolen it originally from Washington Irving's "Salmagundi Papers."
86. Belknap, "Some Notes on Salmagundi," pp. 7-8, 12.
87. Belknap, "Some Notes on Salmagundi," pp. 7-8, 12.
88. Belknap, "Some Notes on Salmagundi," pp. 7-8, 12. Fox was the father of Fontaine Fox, Jr., who became a successful comic strip author. *Kentucky Encyclopedia*, p. 350. Belknap's notes have "F.T. Fox, Jr" as one of the original members of the Salmagundi, but, in fact, the junior Fox wasn't born until five years after the Club was formed.
89. Bodley, Temple. . "Notes on the Origins of the Louisville Park System," pp. 2-3 and Cowan, Andrew. " paper to the Conversation Club," Papers of Temple Bodley (Filson Historical Society) p. 3.
90. Bodley, Temple. "Notes on the Origins of the Louisville Park System," Papers of Temple Bodley, Filson Historical Society, p. 2; Cowan, Andrew. "Paper Read by Colonel Andrew Cowan at a Meeting of the Conversation Club and Also at a Meeting of the Salmagundi Club," *Louisville, KY*, November 14, 1913, Papers of Temple Bodley, Filson Historical Society. Speed was a peripheral member of the prolific clan that had produced James Fry Speed, Abraham Lincoln's best friend, and Joshua Speed, his second attorney general. See Kathleen Jennings, *Louisville's First Families*: a series of genealogical sketches (The Standard Printing Co 1920) pp. 79-88 and John Kleber, ed, *The Louisville Encyclopedia*, (University Press of Kentucky 2001) pp. 842-844. For Cowan, see John Kleber, ed, *The Louisville Encyclopedia*, (University Press of Kentucky 2001) p. 228.
91. Kleber, Louisville Encyclopedia, pp. 842-844. The admiration Cowan's peers held for him is evidenced by the glowing tributes to Cowan such as J. Stoddard Johnston's "Andrew Cowan" essay in *Memorial History of Louisville from Its First Settlement to the Year 1896*, p. 592
92. Cowan, Andrew. "*Paper to the Conversation Club*," November 14, 1913 (Filson Historical Society) p. 3.
93. Bodley, "Notes," p. 3.
94. Bodley, "Notes," p. 3.

95.　"PUBLIC PARKS," *Courier-Journal*
96.　"PUBLIC PARKS," *Courier-Journal*
97.　"PUBLIC PARKS," *Courier-Journal*
98.　"PUBLIC PARKS," *Courier-Journal*
99.　"PUBLIC PARKS," *Courier-Journal*
100.　"PUBLIC PARKS," *Courier-Journal*
101.　"PUBLIC PARKS," *Courier-Journal*
102.　"PUBLIC PARKS," *Courier-Journal*
103.　"PUBLIC PARKS," *Courier-Journal*
104.　Bodley, "Notes," p. 4.
105.　Cowan, "*Paper to the Conversation Club*," p. 3.
106.　Thomas, *Origins*, 114.
107.　"PUBLIC PARKS," *Courier-Journal*
108.　*Encyclopedia of Louisville*, p. 429.
109.　Bodley, "Notes," p. 5 Bodley was a close eye witness, critical and praising of both Jacob and Reed, though as Reed's lawyer he may not have been completely unbiased.
110.　Bodley, "Notes," p. 5; *Encyclopedia of Louisville*, p. 429.
111.　*Encyclopedia of Louisville*, p. 429.
112.　Bodley, "Notes," p. 5
113.　Bodley, "Notes," p. 5
114.　Bodley, "Notes," p. 5
115.　Bodley, "Notes," p. 5
116.　Bodley, "Notes," p. 5
117.　Cowan, "*Paper to the Conversation Club*," p. 3.
118.　Cowan, "*Paper to the Conversation Club*," p. 3.
119.　Cowan, "*Paper to the Conversation Club*," p. 3.
120.　Bodley, history of the park system, p. 12.
121.　Virgin woods are exceedingly rare in the eastern United States. See Bergen, *Forests Forever* p. 29. Burnt Knob was six miles south of Louisville in 1888; now, it is well inside the city boundaries Louisville. See Thomas, Origins, p. 117.
122.　Mann, Charles. 1491: *New Revelations of the Americas before Columbus* (Vintage Books 2006) p. 281.
123.　Mann, *1491*, p. 280.
124.　Mann, *1491*, p. 282.
125.　Mann, *1491*, p. 283.
126.　Bodley, "Notes," p. 12.; *Louisville Encyclopedia*, pp. 198-199.
127.　Cowan, "*Paper to the Conversation Club*," p. 13.
128.　Bodley, "Notes," p. 6.
129.　Bodley, "Notes," p. 6.; See http://www.westegg.com/inflation/infl.cgi for inflation calculations.
130.　See "BEFORE THE COMMITTEE: The Highland-Park Scheme Aired Before Members," *Courier-Journal*, July 7, 1887 (ProQuest Historical Newspapers) and Cowan, Andrew. "Paper to the Conversation Club," November 14, 1913 (Filson Historical Society) p. 1
131.　Bodley, "Notes," p. 6.; See http://www.westegg.com/inflation/infl.cgi for inflation calculations.
132.　Bodley, "Notes," p. 6.
133.　"BEFORE THE COMMITTEE: The Highland-Park Scheme Aired Before Members," *Courier-Journal*, July 7, 1887 (ProQuest Historical Newspapers)
134.　BEFORE THE COMMITTEE: The Highland-Park Scheme Aired Before Members," *Courier-Journal*, July 7, 1887
135.　BEFORE THE COMMITTEE: The Highland-Park Scheme Aired Before Members," *Courier-Journal*, July 7, 1887
136.　Bodley, "Notes," p, pp. 6-7.
137.　Thomas, *Origins*, p. 115
138.　Cowan, "*Paper to the Conversation Club*," p. 13.
139.　Bodley, "Notes," pp. 12-13. Cowan suggests that the Council never named the park Jacob Park, but rather a street car company owned by Jacob's political friends put up signs announcing travel to Jacob Park. However, the Courier-Journal article announcing the park opening states that the Council was going to "christen" the park "Jacob Park." Cowan, " paper to the Conversation Club, p. 15; "JACOB PARK: Picturesque Pleasure Ground to Be Christened in Honor of the Mayor June 1," *Courier-Journal*, May 12, 1889 (ProQuest Historical Newspapers).
140.　Cowan, "*Paper to the Conversation Club*," p. 13.; http://www.westegg.com/inflation/infl.cgi; Thomas, *Origins*, pp. 115-116.
141.　"THE CITY'S NEW PARK: The Beautiful Adornment That Is Taking Place Under the Mayor's Supervision," *Courier-Journal*, May 9, 1889 (ProQuest Historical Newspapers).
142.　Bodley, "Notes," p. 14.
143.　Bodley, "Notes," p. 14.; Cowan, "*Paper to the Conversation Club*," p. 14.
144.　Cowan, "*Paper to the Conversation Club*"
145.　Letter from Henry S. Codman to Frederick Law Olmsted, February 20, 1891, Frederick Law Olmsted Archives, Reel 56 at the Library of Congress.
146.　Letter from Henry S. Codman to Frederick Law Olmsted, February 20, 1891, Frederick Law Olmsted Archives, Reel 56 at the Library of Congress.
147.　Bodley, "Notes on Park History," p. 13. See Thomas, Origins, p. 118.
148.　Cowan, "*Paper to the Conversation Club*," p. 13.
149.　Cowan, "*Paper to the Conversation Club*," p. 13.
150.　Cowan, "*Paper to the Conversation Club*," p. 13.
151.　"JACOB PARK: Picturesque Pleasure Ground to Be Christened in Honor of the Mayor June 1," *Courier-Journal*, May 12, 1889 (ProQuest Historical Newspapers).

152.   *Encyclopedia of Louisville*, pp. 429, 582; Cowan, Paper to the Conversation Club pp. 4-5.
153.   Cowan, *"Paper to the Conversation Club,"* p. 5.
154.   "DOWN CAME THE SNOW: The Muddy Streets Whitened With the First Fall of the Season," *Courier-Journal*, Dec. 17, 1890 (ProQuest Historical Newspapers)
155.   Cowan, *"Paper to the Conversation Club,"* p. 8.
156.   Cowan, *"Paper to the Conversation Club,"* p. 7.
157.   Cowan, *"Paper to the Conversation Club,"* p. 8.
158.   Cowan, *"Paper to the Conversation Club,"* p. 5.
159.   Cowan, *"Paper to the Conversation Club,"* p. 5.
160.   Cowan, *"Paper to the Conversation Club,"* p. 5.
161.   Cowan, *"Paper to the Conversation Club,"* pp. 5-6.
162.   Cowan, *"Paper to the Conversation Club,"* pp. 5-6.
163.   Cowan, *"Paper to the Conversation Club,"* pp. 5-6.
164.   Cowan, *"Paper to the Conversation Club,"* pp. 5-6.
165.   Castleman, *Active Service*, p. 16.
166.   Castleman, *Active Service*, p. 17.
167.   Castleman, *Active Service*, pp. 17, 56.
168.   Castleman, *Active Service*, pp. 53-54.
169.   Castleman, *Active Service*, pp. 15-18.
170.   *The Civil War: Red River to Appomattox* by Shelby Foote (Random House 1974) pp. 359-362.
171.   Castleman, *Active Service*, pp. 172, 191.
172.   Castleman, *Active Service*, pp. 172, 191.
173.   Castleman, *Active Service*, pp. 172, 191.
174.   Bruce Catton, *Bruce Catton's Civil War: Three Volumes in One* (The Fairfax Press, New York) 1984, pp. 621-622.
175.   Castleman, *Active Service*, p. 176.
176.   Letter from Castleman to Hines, from Camp Morton, Indiana, January 1865, Thomas Henry Hines Papers, Filson Historical Society
177.   Castleman, *Active Service*, p. 176.
178.   Castleman, *Active Service*, p. 188.
179.   Letter from Castleman to Hines, from Camp Morton, Indiana, January 1865, Thomas Henry Hines Papers, Filson Historical Society.
180.   Letter from Castleman to Hines, from Camp Morton, Indiana, January 1865, Thomas Henry Hines Papers, Filson Historical Society.
181.   Castleman, *Active Service*, pp. 177-178.
182.   Castleman, *Active Service*, p. 179
183.   Castleman, *Active Service*, p. 179.
184.   Castleman, *Active Service*, p. 179.
185.   Castleman, *Active Service*, p. 179.
186.   Castleman, *Active Service*, p. 179.
187.   Goodwin, *Team of Rivals*, pp. 724-745.
188.   Castleman, *Active Service*, p. 179.
189.   Castleman, *Active Service*, p. 179.
190.   Castleman, *Active Service*, p. 180.
191.   Castleman, *Active Service*, p. 181.
192.   Castleman, *Active Service*, p. 181.
193.   Castleman, *Active Service*, p. 188.
194.   Letter from 17 men to President Andrew Johnson, June 2, 1865, Filson Historical Society. Castleman, *Active Service*, pp. 203-206.
195.   Letter from Castleman to Thomas Henry Hines, Feb. 7, 1867, Filson Historical Society
196.   Cowan, *"Paper to the Conversation Club,"* p. 6.
197.   Cowan, *"Paper to the Conversation Club,"* pp. 6-7
198.   Cowan, *"Paper to the Conversation Club,"* pp. 6-7
199.   Cowan, *"Paper to the Conversation Club,"* pp. 6-7
200.   Cowan, *"Paper to the Conversation Club,"* pp. 6-7
201.   Cowan, *"Paper to the Conversation Club,"* pp. 6-7
202.   Board of Park Commission minutes, July 10, 1890, Minute Book, Louisville Parks & Recreation collection at the Filson Historical Society.
203.   Cowan, *"Paper to the Conversation Club,"* p. 7
204.   Cowan, *"Paper to the Conversation Club,"* p. 7-9
205.   Larson, *The Devil in the White City*, pp. 252-253.
206.   James Klotter, *Kentucky: Portrait in Paradox*, 1900-1950 (Kentucky Historical Society 1996) p. 185. *Confederate Veteran* magazine, from the scrapbook of Enid Yandell, Filson Historical Society, "She has immense physical force, is a trained athlete, rides magnificently, can work sixteen hours a day, and is proud of being the daughter of a Confederate soldier."
207.   James Klotter, *Kentucky: Portrait in Paradox*, 1900-1950 (Kentucky Historical Society 1996) p. 185
208.   Carol Crowe-Carraco, *Women Who Made a Difference* (University Press of Kentucky 1989) p. 30.
209.   Carol Crowe-Carraco, *Women Who Made a Difference* (University Press of Kentucky 1989) p. 30.
210.   Carol Crowe-Carraco, *Women Who Made a Difference* (University Press of Kentucky 1989) p. 30.
211.   Inflation adjustment from http://www.westegg.com/inflation/infl.cgi (accessed 8/5/2015).
212.   James Klotter, *Kentucky: Portrait in Paradox*, 1900-1950 (Kentucky Historical Society 1996) p. 185
213.   Author's observations.
214.   Letter from R.J. Menefee, Jan. 28, 1893, Enid Yandell Papers, Filson Historical Society, Inflation adjustment from http://www.westegg.com/inflation/infl.cgi (accessed 8/5/2015). Yandell's father died when she was 14. Carol Crowe-Carraco, *Women Who Made a Difference*, p. 29.
215.   Larson, *The Devil in the White City*, p. 118.

216. Erik Larson, *The Devil in the White City* (Crown Publishers 2003) pp. 14-15. Larson grippingly chronicles the Exposition and juxtaposes it with a Jack-the-Ripper-like tale of true crime.
217. Larson, *The Devil in the White City*, p. 77.
218. Larson, *The Devil in the White City*, pp. 48-49.
219. Rybczinski, *Clearing in the Distance*, pp. 376, 423-424; Larson, Devil in the White City, pp. 51, 53.
220. Larson, *The Devil in the White City*, pp. 53, 143.
221. Larson, *The Devil in the White City*, pp. 49, 332.
222. Olmsted, *Essential Texts*, p. 100.
223. Larson, *The Devil in the White City*, pp. 51-52; http://www.westegg.com/inflation/infl.cgi
224. Larson, *The Devil in the White City*, p. 121.
225. Larson, *The Devil in the White City*, p. 53.
226. Larson, *The Devil in the White City*, p. 194.; Martin, Genius, pp. 344-345, 382.
227. Larson, *The Devil in the White City*, pp. 52-53, 167.
228. Rybczinski, *Clearing in the Distance*, p. 386.
229. Larson, *The Devil in the White City*, pp. 116, 143.
230. Rybczinski, *Clearing in the Distance*, pp. 386, 389.
231. Rybczinksi, *Clearing in the Distance*, p. 386.
232. Rybczinski, *Clearing in the Distance*, p. 386.
233. Though, of course, the drawing didn't hurt. Rybczinski, *Clearing in the Distance*, p. 170.
234. Letter from FLO to FLO, Jr., August 1, 1895, Frederick Law Olmsted Archive at LOC, Reel 23.
235. Letter from FLO to Van Brunt, Jan. 22, 1891, FLO Reel 22 LOC
236. Letter from FLO to Van Brunt, Jan. 22, 1891, FLO Reel 22 LOC
237. Letter from FLO to Van Brunt, Jan. 22, 1891, FLO Reel 22 LOC
238. Martin, *Genius*, p. 378.
239. See, for example, the famous photograph of Olmsted looking like a cherubic genius Santa Claus versus the portrait of him at Biltmore by John Singer Sargent.
240. Concise Oxford English Dictionary, Catherine Soanes and Angus Stevenson, Eds. (Oxford University Press 2006) p. 962.
241. Larson, *The Devil in the White City*, p. 51. For Beethoven's tinnitus, see Edmund Morris, *Beethoven: Universal Composer* (Harper Collins, 2005).
242. Rybczynski, *Clearing*, pp. 248, 316, 335, 337-338.
243. Larson, *The Devil in the White City*, p. 194.
244. Martin, *Genius*, pp. 173, 341. Olmsted and Mary's first son, John Theodore, had died as a three-month-old from cholera, and his other stepson/nephew Owen had died at age 24 from tuberculosis.
245. Letter from Frederick Law "Rick" Olmsted, Jr. to Frederick Law Olmsted, Sr., June 24, 1891, LOC, FLO Archive, Reel 22.
246. Rybczynski, *Clearing in the Distance*, p. 334.
247. Rybczynski, *Clearing in the Distance*, pp. 334-335.
248. Many if not most of the Olmsted Associates Archive and FLO Archive letters at the Library of Congress have stamps and initials noting who received the letter, who read it, who acknowledged it.
249. Larson, *The Devil in the White City*, p. 276.
250. Larson, *The Devil in the White City*, p. 276.
251. Castleman, *Castleman, Active Service*, p. 217
252. Larson, *The Devil in the White City*, pp. 252-253.
253. Rybczinksi, *Clearing in the Distance*, p. 393.; Larson, *The Devil in the White City*, pp. 218-220.
254. Larson, *The Devil in the White City*, p. 220
255. Rybczinksi, *Clearing in the Distance*, p. 394.
256. Larson, *The Devil in the White City*, p. 220.
257. Rybczinksi, *Clearing in the Distance*, p. 394.
258. Letter from A.G. del Campillo to Mrs. Durrett (wife of R.T. Durrett), Oct. 31, 1893, Filson Historical Society, papers of R.T. Durrett
259. Larson, *Devil in the White City*, p. 335.
260. Image ULPA 1998.09.153 Martin F. Schmidt Photographs of Louisville, ca. 1956-1966, 1998.09, Photographic Archives, University of Louisville, Louisville, Kentucky. http://digital.library.louisville.edu/cdm/singleitem/collection/schmidt/id/127/rec/30 (accessed March 14, 2015).
261. Letter from Cowan to Olmsted, Louisville, January 3, 1891, Olmsted Associates Archive, Reel 60, Library of Congress.
262. Letter from Cowan to Olmsted, Louisville, January 3, 1891, Olmsted Associates Archive, Reel 60, Library of Congress.
263. Cowan, *"Paper to the Commercial Club,"* p. 16.
264. Letter from Andrew Cowan to Frederick Law Olmsted, January 8, 1891, Olmsted Associates Archive at the Library of Congress, Reel 60.
265. Letter from Cowan to Olmsted, January 22, 1891, Olmsted Associates, LOC, Reel 60
266. Letter from Andrew Cowan to Frederick Law Olmsted, January 22, 1891, Olmsted Associates, LOC, Reel 60.; See Bodley, "Notes on Parks," p. 15, discussing the park bill having been "mutilated" and then the mutilating amendments withdrawn.
267. Letter from Andrew Cowan to Frederick Law Olmsted, January 22, 1891, Olmsted Associates, LOC, Reel 60.
268. Thomas, *Origins*, pp. 138-139.
269. Letter from Henry Codman to Frederick Law Olmsted, read by John C. Olmsted, February 20, 1891, FLO Archive, Reel 56
270. Letter from Henry Codman to Frederick Law Olmsted, Feb. 20, 1891, FLO Archive, Reel 56
271. Letter from Henry Codman to Frederick Law Olmsted, Feb. 20, 1891, FLO Archive, Reel 56
272. Letter from Henry Codman to Frederick Law Olmsted, Feb. 20, 1891, FLO Archive, Reel 56
273. Letter from Henry Codman to Frederick Law Olmsted, Feb. 20, 1891, FLO Archive, Reel 56
274. Letter from Henry Codman to Frederick Law Olmsted, Feb. 20, 1891, FLO Archive, Reel 56
275. Letter from F.L.O. & Co. to Thomas Sherley, February 26, 1891, Olmsted Associates Archive, LOC, Reel 60
276. Letter from Andrew Cowan to Frederick Law Olmsted & Co, March 17, 1891, Olmsted Associates Archive, LOC, Reel 60

277. Letter from Andrew Cowan to Frederick Law Olmsted & Co, March 17, 1891, Olmsted Associates Archive, LOC, Reel 60
278. Letter from Sherley to Messrs. F.L. Olmsted & Co., April 17, 1891, LOC, Olmsted Associates Archive, Reel 60.
279. Cowan, "*Paper to the Commercial Club,*" p. 8.
280. Cowan, "*Paper to the Commercial Club,*" pp. 7-9.
281. Cowan, "*Paper to the Commercial Club,*" p. 9.
282. Cowan, "*Paper to the Commercial Club,*" pp. 9-10.
283. Letter from Olmsted to Fred Kingsley, January 20, 1891, Frederick Law Olmsted archive, Library of Congress, Reel 22.
284. Letter from Olmsted to Fred Kingsley, January 20, 1891, Frederick Law Olmsted archive, Library of Congress, Reel 22.
285. Letter from FLO to JCO, Mar. 13, 1894, LOC FLO Reel 23.
286. Letter from FLO to JCO, Mar. 13, 1894, LOC FLO Reel 23.
287. Letter from Olmsted to Fred Kingsley, January 20, 1891, Frederick Law Olmsted archive, Library of Congress, Reel 22.
288. "The Public Parks and Parkways," Andrew Cowan, *Memorial History of Louisville from Its First Settlement to the Year 1896*, edited by J. Stoddard Johnston, (American Biographical Publishing Co. 1896) p. 343
289. Frederick Law Olmsted, *The Louisville Times*, May 21, 1891.
290. "LAYING OUT THE PARKS: The Wisdom of the Commissioners In Selecting the Best Landscape Architects Heartily Indorsed," *Courier-Journal*, May 24, 1891 (ProQuest Historical Newspapers).
291. Letter to from Andrew Cowan to R.T. Durrett, signed "RHP," May 20, 1891, Papers of R.T. Durrett, Filson Historical Society.
292. "CHOSE THE OLD OFFICERS," *Courier-Journal*, Nov. 3, 1891 (ProQuest Historical Newspapers). *The Louisville Encyclopedia*, pp. 696-697.
293. "THE PENDENNIS CLUB," *Courier-Journal*, Nov. 5, 1890 (ProQuest Historical Newspapers)
294. "THE PENDENNIS CLUB," *Courier-Journal*, Nov. 5, 1890 (ProQuest Historical Newspapers)
295. Letter from C.S. Collings to R.T. Durrett, January 20, 1892, Filson Historical Society, Papers of R.T. Durrett
296. "PARK COMMISSIONERS," *Courier-Journal*, Jul. 8, 1890 (ProQuest Historical Newspapers).
297. R.T. Durrett papers, Filson
298. Cowan, Public Parks article
299. R.T. Durrett, a fellow Salmagundian, Park Commissioner, and founder of the Filson Historical Society wrote to several cities asking for information on their public parks: Boston, Philadelphia, Buffalo, Brooklyn, Washington, D.C.,
300. Erik Larson, *Devil in the White City*, p. 322.
301. Report from firm to Thomas H. Sherley, August 26th 1891.
302. Report from FL Olmsted & Co. to Thomas H. Sherley, president of the Louisville Board of Park Commissioners, August 26th 1891. The report summarizes extemporaneous remarks Olmsted had given to the Louisville Board of Park Commissioners. It isn't signed by Olmsted, and it's quite possible that there were contributions to the formal report made by members of Olmsted's staff. Nevertheless, the writing has the unmistakable ring of Frederick Law Olmsted. The report is in his voice.
303. Letter from F.L. Olmsted & Co. to Thomas H. Sherley, August 26th, 1891, LOC, Olmsted Associates Archive, Reel 60.
304. Letter from F.L. Olmsted & Co. to Thomas H. Sherley, August 26th, 1891, LOC, Olmsted Associates Archive, Reel 60.
305. Letter from F.L. Olmsted & Co. to Thomas H. Sherley, August 26th, 1891, LOC, Olmsted Associates Archive, Reel 60.
306. Letter from F.L. Olmsted & Co. to Thomas H. Sherley, August 26th, 1891, LOC, Olmsted Associates Archive, Reel 60.
307. Thomas, *Origins*, p. 141.
308. Thomas, *Origins*, p. 141.
309. The Galt House building where Olmsted stayed still stands at 600 West Main Street in downtown Louisville, just upbank from the river.
310. FLO to JCO, July 25, 1891, LOC, Frederick Law Olmsted Archive, Reel 22.
311. FLO to JCO, July 25, 1891, LOC, Frederick Law Olmsted Archive, Reel 22; Rybczynski, *Clearing*, p. 335.
312. FLO to JCO, July 25, 1891, LOC, Frederick Law Olmsted Archive, Reel 22.
313. "PARKS TO BE NAMED," *Courier-Journal*, Aug. 13, 1891 (ProQuest Historical Newspapers)
314. "GIVEN INDIAN NAMES," *Courier-Journal*, Aug. 14, 1891 (ProQuest Historical Newspapers)
315. "GIVEN INDIAN NAMES," *Courier-Journal*, Aug. 14, 1891 (ProQuest Historical Newspapers)
316. "GIVEN INDIAN NAMES," *Courier-Journal*, Aug. 14, 1891 (ProQuest Historical Newspapers)
317. "IROQUOIS PARK," *Courier-Journal*, Aug. 14, 1891 (ProQuest Historical Newspapers)
318. Even New York had lacked sufficient "pleasure drives" before Olmsted and Vaux got involved. Olmsted, *Essential Texts*, p. 248.
319. Cowan, *Public Parks*, CJ
320. Olmsted, *Essential Texts*, p. 232.
321. Thomas, *Origins*, p. 145.
322. Olmsted, *Essential Texts*, p. 319
323. Olmsted, *Essential Texts*, p. 232.
324. Thomas, *Origins*, p. 145.
325. "A WESTERN PARK: The Commissioners Likely to Purchase Fountain Ferry Farm," *Courier-Journal*, May 22, 1891.
326. Thomas, *Origins*, p. 144.
327. Thomas, *Origins*, p. 146.
328. Arleyn A. Levee, *Louisville's Olmsted Park Legacy: Selective Chronology* (Olmsted Parks Conservancy 1992) pp. 3-5.
329. Letter from Andrew Cowan to Harry Codman, April 9, 1892, LOC, Olmsted Associates Archive, Reel 60 and Arleyn A. Levee, *Louisville's Olmsted Park Legacy: Selective Chronology* (Olmsted Parks Conservancy 1992) pp. 4-5.
330. Letter from Andrew Cowan to Harry Codman, April 9, 1892, LOC, Olmsted Associates Archive, Reel 60.
331. Thomas, *Origins*, pp. 141, 316. Letter from Cowan to F.L. Olmsted & Co., March 26, 1892, Olmsted Associates Archive, LOC, Reel 60.
332. Letter from Andrew Cowan to Harry Codman, April 9, 1892, LOC, Olmsted Associates Archive, Reel 60.
333. Beveridge ed, letter from FLO & Co. to E. Mahlo, March 1, 1892, Olmsted Documentary Resource, p. 97.
334. Martin, *Genius*, p. 378.
335. Letter from FLO to JCO, April 20, 1892, LOC, FLO Archive, Reel 22.
336. Letter from FLO to JCO, April 20, 1892, LOC, FLO Archive, Reel 22.
337. Letter from FLO to JCO, April 20, 1892, LOC, FLO Archive, Reel 22.

338.   Letter from FLO to Harry Codman, Chislehurst, England, Apr. 21, 1892, LOC FLO Archive, Reel 22.
339.   Letter from FLO to Harry Codman, Chislehurst, England, Apr. 21, 1892, LOC FLO Archive, Reel 22.
340.   Letter from FLO to Harry Codman, Chislehurst, England, Apr. 21, 1892, LOC FLO Archive, Reel 22.
341.   Letter from FLO to JCO and HSC, Apr. 29, 1892, LOC FLO Archive, Reel 22.
342.   Letter from FLO to JCO and HSC, Apr. 29, 1892, LOC FLO Archive, Reel 22.
343.   Beveridge ed, letter from FLO & Co. to Thomas Sherley, Apr. 26, 1892, Olmsted Documentary Resource, p. 116.
344.   Beveridge ed, letter from FLO & Co. to Thomas Sherley, Apr. 26, 1892, Olmsted Documentary Resource, p. 116.
345.   Beveridge ed, letter from FLO & Co. to Thomas Sherley, Apr. 26, 1892, Olmsted Documentary Resource, p. 116.
346.   Thomas, *Origins*, p. 151.
347.   Letter from Thomas Sherley to F.L. Olmsted & Co, Apr. 29, 1892, LOC, Olmsted Associates Archive, Reel 60.
348.   Telegram from Cowan and Mahlo to Codman, May 14, 1892, LOC Olmsted Associates Archive, Reel 60.
349.   Beveridge ed, Letter from F.L. Olmsted & Co. to Mahlo, Aug. 3, 1892, Olmsted Documentary Resource, p. 100.
350.   Letter from FLO to HSC, Chislehurst, England, May 25, 1892, LOC FLO Archive, Reel 41.
351.   Letter from FLO to HSC, Chislehurst, England, May 25, 1892, LOC FLO Archive, Reel 41.
352.   Letter from F.L. Olmsted & Co. to J.H. Willard, Jun. 4, 1892, LOC FLO Archive, Reel 22.
353.   Letter from FLO to HSC, Jun. 16, 1892, LOC FLO Reel 22.
354.   Letter from FLO to HSC, Jun. 16, 1892, LOC FLO Reel 22.
355.   Letter from FLO to "partners," July 1892, Hampstead, LOC FLO Archive, Reel 22.
356.   Letter from FLO to "partners," July 1892, Hampstead, LOC FLO Archive, Reel 22.
357.   Letter from FLO to JCO, Oct. 1, 1892, LOC FLO Reel 22.
358.   Letter from FLO to JCO, Jul. 26, 1892, LOC FLO Archive, Reel 22.
359.   Letter from FLO to HSC, Jul. 30, 1892, LOC FLO Archive, Reel 22.
360.   "PRESIDENT CASTLEMAN: Park Commissioners Elect Col. Castleman President of the Board," *Courier-Journal*, Aug. 3, 1892 (ProQuest Historical Newspapers).
361.   Official Minutes of the Board of Park Commissioners, Aug. 16, 1892, Filson Historical Society, p. 60.
362.   Official Minutes of the Board of Park Commissioners, Aug. 16, 1892, Filson Historical Society, p. 60.
363.   FLO & Co to Cowan, August 22, 1892. Olmsted Documentary Resource (Beveridge and Levee, eds).
364.   FLO & Co to Cowan, August 22, 1892. Olmsted Documentary Resource (Beveridge and Levee, eds).
365.   JBC to firm, August 25, 1892, OA Reel 60.
366.   JBC to firm, August 29, 1892, OA Reel 60
367.   JBC to firm, August 29, 1892, OA Reel 60
368.   Letter from FLO to JCO, Aug. 25, 1892, LOC FLO Archive, Reel 22.
369.   Larson, *Devil*, p. 179.
370.   Larson, *Devil*, p. 179.
371.   Letter from FLO to JCO, Oct. 3, 1892, LOC FLO Archive, Reel 22.
372.   Letter from Cowan to F.L. Olmsted & Co., Aug. 29, 1892, LOC Olmsted Associates Archive, Reel 60.
373.   Letter from Cowan to F.L. Olmsted & Co., Aug. 29, 1892, LOC Olmsted Associates Archive, Reel 60.
374.   Letter from Cowan to F.L. Olmsted & Co., Aug. 29, 1892, LOC Olmsted Associates Archive, Reel 60.
375.   Letter from FLO to JCO, Oct. 11, 1892, Chicago, LOC FLO Archive, Reel 22.
376.   Letter from FLO to JCO, Oct. 11, 1892, Chicago, LOC FLO Archive, Reel 22.
377.   Thomas, *Origins*, pp. 163-165.
378.   Larson, *Devil*, pp. 192, 194; Rybczynski, *Clearing*, p. 392.
379.   Letter from FLO to Gifford Pinchot, Jan. 19, 1893, LOC FLO Archive, Reel 22.
380.   Letter from FLO to JCO from Chicago, Feb. 4, 1893.
381.   Letter from FLO to JCO from Chicago, Feb 6, 1893.
382.   Letter from FLO to JCO from Chicago, Feb. 17, 1893.
383.   Louisville made Olmsted's list of "matters of chief importance" and Cherokee Park his list "more noticeable public works performed, formed, or forming mainly upon plans devised by Mr. Olmsted in association with an or another of their other landscape architects: Calvert Vaux, J.C. Olmsted, H.S. Codman, Charles Eliot." Letter from FLO to JCO, June 13, 1893, FLO Reel 22, LOC. Letter from FLO to JCO from Chicago, Feb. 17, 1893.
384.   Martin, *Genius*, pp. 344-345, 382.
385.   Letter from FLO to JCO from Chicago, Feb. 17, 1893 and Rybczinski, *Clearing in the Distance*, p. 409.
386.   Martin, *Genius*, p. 382
387.   Cowan, "Paper to the Commercial Club", p. 16.
388.   Thomas, *Origins*, pp. 155-156.
389.   Cowan, "Paper to the Commercial Club", p. 12.
390.   Cowan, "Paper to the Commercial Club", p. 12.
391.   Cowan, "Paper to the Commercial Club", p. 12. and "A West-End Park," *The Courier-Journal*, Jun. 10, 1891 (ProQuest Historical Newspapers).
392.   Cowan, "Paper to the Commercial Club", p. 12.
393.   Cowan, "Paper to the Commercial Club", p. 12.
394.   "A West-End Park," *The Courier-Journal*, Jun. 10, 1891 (ProQuest Historical Newspapers).
395.   Thomas, *Origins*, pp. 155-156.
396.   Thomas, *Origins*, pp. 155-156. Letter from FLO & Co to JBC, Nov. 17, 1892, *Olmsted Documentary Resource* and Letter from FLO & Co to JBC, Nov. 17, 1892, LOC FLO collection, Reel 22.
397.   Letter from FLO & Co to JBC, Nov. 17, 1892, *Olmsted Documentary Resource*
398.   "OSTRICH FOR WESTERN PARK," *Courier-Journal*, Dec. 10, 1892 (ProQuest Historical Newspapers).
399.   Letter from FLO to JCO from Milwaukee, Feb 10, 1893.
400.   Cowan, "Paper to the Commercial Club", p. 13.

401. Artemas Richardson and Joseph Hudak, *Journal of the Development of Cherokee Park, 1891-1974*, (Olmsted Associates, Inc. 1974), p. 20.
402. Artemas Richardson and Joseph Hudak, *Journal of the Development of Cherokee Park, 1891-1974*, (Olmsted Associates, Inc. 1974), pp. 20-21.
403. Arleyn A. Levee, *Louisville's Olmsted Park Legacy: Selective Chronology* (Olmsted Parks Conservancy 1992) p. 7
404. Arleyn A. Levee, *Louisville's Olmsted Park Legacy: Selective Chronology* (Olmsted Parks Conservancy 1992) pp. 7-8
405. Letter from FLO to JCO, Apr. 24, 1893, FLO Archive Reel 22, LOC.
406. Letter from Eliot to JBC, Apr. 29, 1893, OA Archive, Reel 60, LOC
407. Letter from Eliot to FLO, May 31, 1893, LOC FLO Reel 22
408. Letter from FLO to JCO, Nov. 1, 1893, FLO Reel 23, LOC
409. Letter from FLO to JCO, Nov. 1, 1893, FLO Reel 23, LOC
410. Letter from FLO to JCO, Nov. 1, 1893, FLO Reel 23, LOC
411. Letter from FLO to JCO, Nov. 1, 1893, FLO Reel 23, LOC
412. Letter from FLO to JCO, Oct. 28, 1893, FLO Reel 23, LOC. See also, Letter from FLO o JCO, Nov. 8, 1893, Reel 23, LOC.
413. Letter from FLO to JCO, Oct. 27, 1893, FLO Reel 23, LOC
414. Letter from FLO to JCO, Oct. 27, 1893, FLO Reel 23, LOC
415. Letter from FLO to JCO, Nov. 23, 1893, FLO Reel 23, LOC
416. Letter from FLO to JCO, Nov. 26, 1893, FLO Archive, Reel 23, LOC. "I shall not mind having a day or two to spare at Louisville, having to think out some matters," he wrote to John.
417. Letter from FLO to JCO, Apr. 24, 1893, FLO Archive Reel 22, LOC.
418. Letter from FLO to Eliot, Feb. 21, 1894, FLO Archive, Reel 23, LOC.
419. Letter from FLO to Eliot, Feb. 21, 1894, FLO Archive, Reel 23, LOC.
420. Letter from FLO to JCO, Mar. 15, 1894, LOC FLO Reel 23
421. Letter from FLO to JCO, Mar. 13, 1894, LOC FLO Reel 23.
422. Letter from FLO to JCO, Mar. 15, 1894, LOC FLO Reel 23
423. Letter from FLO to Eliot, Mar. 20, 1894, LOC FLO Reel 23
424. Letter from Eliot to FLO, Jul. 25, 1894, LOC Reel 23
425. Letter from Eliot to FLO, Jul. 25, 1894, LOC Reel 23
426. Letter from Eliot to FLO, Jul. 25, 1894, LOC Reel 23
427. Letter from FLO to William A. Stiles, Sep. 18, 1894, FLO Reel 23
428. Martin, *Genius*, pp. 379-380.
429. Letter from FLO to Stiles, Sep. 18, 1894, FLO Reel 23
430. Letter from FLO to Stiles, Sep. 18, 1894, FLO Reel 23
431. Letter from FLO to Calvert Vaux, Summer 1894, FLO Archives at LOC, Reel 23
432. Letter from FLO to FLO, Jr., Jan. 7, 1895, FLO Archives at LOC, Reel 23.
433. Letter from FLO to FLO, Jr., Jan. 15, 1895, FLO Archives at LOC, Reel 23.
434. Letter from FLO to FLO, Jr., Jan. 15, 1895, FLO Archives at LOC, Reel 23.
435. Letter from FLO to Partners, Mar. 13, 1895, FLO Archives at LOC, Reel 23.
436. Justin Martin, *Genius of Place* (Da Capo Press 2011) p. 392.
437. Rybczynski, *Clearing in the Distance*, p. 405.
438. Letter from FLO to JCO, May 10, 1895 from Biltmore, FLO Archives at LOC, Reel 23
439. Letter from FLO to JCO, May 10, 1895 from Biltmore, FLO Archives at LOC, Reel 23
440. Letter from FLO to JCO, May 10, 1895 from Biltmore, FLO Archives at LOC, Reel 23
441. Letter from FLO to JCO, May 10, 1895 from Biltmore, FLO Archives at LOC, Reel 23
442. Letter from George Vanderbilt to Olmsted, FLO Archive LOC, Reel 23
443. Rybczynski, *Clearing in the Distance*, p. 405.
444. Letter from FLO to FLO, Jr., July or August 11, 1895, FLO Archive LOC Reel 23.
445. Letter from FLO to FLO, Jr., July or August 11, 1895, FLO Archive LOC Reel 23.
446. Letter from FLO to FLO, Jr., July or August 11, 1895, FLO Archive LOC Reel 23.
447. Letter from FLO to FLO, Jr., Aug. 1, 1895, FLO Archives LOC Reel 23.
448. Letter from FLO to FLO, Jr., July 23, 1895, FLO Archives LOC Reel 23.
449. Letter from FLO to FLO, Jr., July 23, 1895, FLO Archives LOC Reel 23.
450. Letter from FLO to FLO, Jr., July 23, 1895, FLO Archives LOC Reel 23.
451. Letter from FLO to FLO, Jr., Aug. 1, 1895, FLO Archives LOC Reel 23.
452. Letter from FLO to FLO, Jr., Aug. 1, 1895, FLO Archives LOC Reel 23.
453. Letter from FLO to FLO, Jr., Aug. 1, 1895, FLO Archives LOC Reel 23.
454. Letter from FLO to FLO, Jr., July or August 11, 1895, FLO Archive LOC Reel 23. Rybczynski, *A Clearing in the Distance*, p. 410. Thomas, Origins, p. 167.
455. Letter from FLO to FLO Jr, Aug. 13, 1895, FLO Archives LOC Reel 23.
456. Letter from FLO to FLO Jr, Oct. 14, 1895, FLO Archives LOC Reel 23.
457. Letter from FLO to FLO Jr, Oct. 15, 1895, FLO Archives LOC Reel 23
458. Letter from FLO to FLO, Jr., undated but referencing FLO Jr letter of Oct. 5, FLO Archives LOC Reel 23.
459. Letter from FLO to FLO Jr, Nov. 7, 1895, FLO Archives LOC Reel 23
460. Letter from FLO to FLO Jr, Nov. 7, 1895, FLO Archives LOC Reel 23
461. Justin Martin, *Genius of Place* (Da Capo Press 2011) pp. 366-367.
462. Justin Martin, *Genius of Place* (Da Capo Press 2011) pp. 366-367.
463. Justin Martin, *Genius of Place* (Da Capo Press 2011) pp. 366-367.
464. Justin Martin, *Genius of Place* (Da Capo Press 2011) pp. 366-367.
465. Rybczynski, *Clearing*, pp. 410-411.
466. Rybczynski, *Clearing*, pp. 410-411.

467. Letter from George Vanderbilt to JCO, Sep. 9, 1903. LOC FLO Archive Reel 23.
468. Letter from Édouard Andre to Olmsted Brothers, Sep. 21, 1903, LOC FLO Archive, Reel 23.
469. Rybczynski, *Clearing*, p. 411.
470. Letter from Louisville Board of Park Commissioners to Olmsted Bros. Oct. 20, 1903, LOC FLO Archive, Reel 23.
471. 472 Letter from Louisville Board of Park Commissioners to Olmsted Bros, Oct. 20, 1903, LOC FLO Archive, Reel 23.
472. "The Public Parks and Parkways," Andrew Cowan, *Memorial History of Louisville from Its First Settlement to the Year 1896*, edited by J. Stoddard Johnston, (American Biographical Publishing Co. 1896) p. 343.
473. "The Public Parks and Parkways," Andrew Cowan, *Memorial History of Louisville from Its First Settlement to the Year 1896*, edited by J. Stoddard Johnston, (American Biographical Publishing Co. 1896) p. 343.
474. "The Public Parks and Parkways," Andrew Cowan, *Memorial History of Louisville from Its First Settlement to the Year 1896*, edited by J. Stoddard Johnston, (American Biographical Publishing Co. 1896) pp. 342-343.
475. "The Public Parks and Parkways," Andrew Cowan, *Memorial History of Louisville from Its First Settlement to the Year 1896*, edited by J. Stoddard Johnston, (American Biographical Publishing Co. 1896) pp. 343.
476. "The Public Parks and Parkways," Andrew Cowan, *Memorial History of Louisville from Its First Settlement to the Year 1896*, edited by J. Stoddard Johnston, (American Biographical Publishing Co. 1896) pp. 343.
477. Letter from JCO to Mary Olmsted, Apr. 24, 1896, LOC FLO Reel 23.
478. Beveridge ed, letter from FLO & Co. to Andrew Cowan, May 4, 1892, Olmsted Documentary Resource, p. 31.
479. Letter from Olmsted, Olmsted & Eliot to JBC, April 1, 1895, "Journal of the Development of Cherokee Park, Louisville, Kentucky, 1891-1974" Olmsted Associates, p. 26.
480. Letter from JCO to Mary Olmsted, Apr. 24, 1896, LOC FLO Reel 23.
481. Letter from JCO to Mary Olmsted, Apr. 24, 1896, LOC FLO Reel 23.
482. Letter from JCO to FLO, Jr., Apr. 16, 1896, LOC FLO Archive Reel 23.
483. Letter from JCO to FLO, Jr., Apr. 24, 1896, LOC FLO Archive Reel 23.
484. Letter from JCO to Mary Olmsted, Apr. 24, 1896, LOC FLO Reel 23.
485. Letter from JCO to FLO, Jr., Apr. 24, 1896, LOC FLO Archive Reel 23.
486. Letter from JCO to FLO, Jr., Nov. 6, 1895, FLO Archives LOC Reel 23. The hourly rate was $1,200 a year. West Egg Inflation Calculator for inflation adjustment, accessed Sep. 3, 2015.
487. Letter from JCO to FLO, Jr., Nov. 6, 1895, FLO Archives LOC Reel 23. The hourly rate was $1,200 a year.
488. Letter from Kinkead to OO&E, Mar. 12, 1896, LOC Olmsted Associates Archive, Reel 60.
489. Letter from Kinkead to OO&E, Mar. 12, 1896, LOC Olmsted Associates Archive, Reel 60.
490. Letter from Kinkead to OO&E, Mar. 12, 1896, LOC Olmsted Associates Archive, Reel 60.
491. Letter from JCO to JBC, Apr. 16, 1896, LOC Olmsted Associates Reel 60.
492. Letter from JCO to JBC, Apr. 16, 1896, LOC Olmsted Associates Reel 60.
493. Letter from JCO to Kinkead, Apr. 26, 1896, LOC Olmsted Associates Reel 60.
494. Letter from JCO to Robert Kinkead, Apr. 17, 1896, LOC Olmsted Associates Reel 60.
495. Letter from JCO to Robert Kinkead, Apr. 17, 1896, LOC Olmsted Associates Reel 60.
496. "THE MAINE MYSTERY," Feb 17, 1898, *Courier-Journal* (ProQuest Historical Newspapers)
497. "DECLARATION OF WAR," Apr 24, 1898, *Courier-Journal* (ProQuest Historical Newspapers)
498. *Encyclopedia of Louisville*, p. 163.
499. Castleman, *Active Service*, pp. 219-220.
500. Castleman, *Active Service*, pp. 219-220.
501. Castleman, *Active Service*, pp. 222-223.
502. Letter from Warren Manning to Olmsted, Olmsted & Eliot, Aug. 1, 1896, LOC Olmsted Associates Reel 60.; "SAVING PONCE'S TREES: COL. CASTLEMAN DENOUNCES WORK OF SIGNAL CORPS," Nov 29, 1898 ProQuest Historical Newspapers: Louisville Courier Journal
503. SAVING PONCE'S TREES: COL. CASTLEMAN DENOUNCES WORK OF SIGNAL CORPS," Nov 29, 1898 ProQuest Historical Newspapers: Louisville *Courier-Journal*.
504. Diary of William Onderdonk, Filson Historical Society
505. William Onderdonk papers, The Filson Historical Society
506. William Onderdonk papers, The Filson Historical Society
507. William Onderdonk papers, The Filson Historical Society
508. Letter from W.T. Rolph to JBC, Jan. 11, 1899, Filson Historical Society
509. Rebecca Summer, "Partnership for a Democratic Society: Frederick Law Olmsted, Andrew Cowan, and the Louisville Park System," Yale Thesis, April 2010, p. 59.
510. Letter from JCO to JBC, Apr. 17, 1896, "Journal of the Development of Cherokee Park, Louisville, Kentucky, 1891-1974" Olmsted Associates, pp. 29, 32.
511. Journal entry of JCO, Feb. 3, 1907, LOC Olmsted Associates, Reel 61.
512. *Encyclopedia of Louisville*, p. 896. Notes of JCO, Feb. 3, 1907, LOC OA Reel 61
513. Notes of JCO, Feb. 3, 1907, LOC OA Reel 61
514. Notes of JCO, Feb. 3, 1907, LOC OA Reel 61
515. Letter from JCO to JBC, Dec. 6, 1907, LOC Olmsted Associates Archive, Reel 61. Thomas, *Origins*, p. 204.
516. Inventory and Appraisement of Castleman Estate, Sep. 17, 1918, Second Folder, Filson Historical Society.
517. Inventory and Appraisement of Castleman Estate, Sep. 17, 1918, Second Folder, Filson Historical Society.
518. "Louisville System of Parks Admittedly Among the Best In the World," Nov. 7, 1917, *Courier-Journal*, (ProQuest Historical Newspapers).
519. "Louisville System of Parks Admittedly Among the Best In the World," Nov. 7, 1917, *Courier-Journal*, (ProQuest Historical Newspapers).
520. "Louisville System of Parks Admittedly Among the Best In the World," Nov. 7, 1917, *Courier-Journal*, (ProQuest Historical Newspapers).
521. For Shawnee, see Thomas, *Origins*, pp. 158-159.
522. "Louisville System of Parks Admittedly Among the Best In the World," Nov. 7, 1917, *Courier-Journal*, (ProQuest Historical Newspapers).
523. "10,000 CROWD IN TYLER PARK," *Courier-Journal*, Jul. 6, 1915 (ProQuest Historical Newspapers).

524. Thomas, *Origins*, pp. 160-162.

525. FIFTY THOUSAND DO HONOR TO KENTUCKY'S BACK WOODS MAN," Jun 16, 1906, *Courier-Journal* (ProQuest Historical Newspapers).

526. "Countrymen Pay Tribute To Gen. John B. Castleman At Unveiling of His Statue Near Cherokee Park," Nov. 9, 1913, *Courier-Journal* (ProQuest Historical Newspapers)

527. "LARGE CROWD EXPECTED TO SEE CASTLEMAN UNVEILING," Nov 8, 1913, *Courier-Journal* (ProQuest Historical Newspapers)

528. "BEAUTY OF CITY PARKS PRAISED," John B. Castleman and D.F. Murphy, *Courier-Journal*, Nov. 20, 1917 (ProQuest Historical Newspapers)

529. See "List of Parks by Total Acreage," NYC.gov, www1.nyc.gov/assets/buildings/excel/dpr_park_list.xls; "Current Population Estimates," http://www1.nyc.gov/site/planning/data-maps/nyc-population/current-future-populations.page; US Census Bureau American Community Surveys

530. See Olmsted Parks Conservancy, http://www.olmstedparks.org/our-parks

531. See Louisville Metro Parks, https://louisvilleky.gov/government/jefferson-memorial-forest/about-jefferson-memorial-forest

532. See parklands.org/21st-century-parks.html

533. "SEGREGATION OF RACE IS URGED: W. D. Binford Asks Enactment of Ordinance" Nov. 15, 1913; *Courier-Journal* (ProQuest Historical Newspapers).

534. "SEGREGATION OF RACE IS URGED: W. D. Binford Asks Enactment of Ordinance" Nov. 15, 1913; *Courier-Journal* (ProQuest Historical Newspapers).

535. "SEGREGATION OF RACE IS URGED: W. D. Binford Asks Enactment of Ordinance" Nov. 15, 1913; *Courier-Journal* (ProQuest Historical Newspapers).

536. "SEGREGATION OF RACE IS URGED: W. D. Binford Asks Enactment of Ordinance" Nov. 15, 1913; *Courier-Journal* (ProQuest Historical Newspapers).

537. Rebecca Summer, "Partnership for a Democratic Society: Frederick Law Olmsted, Andrew Cowan, and the Louisville Park System," Yale Thesis, April 2010, pp. 57-58.

538. THE MAYSVILLE LYNCHING: A Protest Against the Feeling Attributed To the ''Better People," C E Craik, Dec 14, 1899, *Courier-Journal* (ProQuest Historical Newspapers)

539. "LYNCHING FEARED," *Courier-Journal*, Jan. 9, 1904 (ProQuest Historical Newspapers)

540. "The Ku Klux Klan in the 1920s," http://www.pbs.org/wgbh/americanexperience/features/general-article/flood-klan/

541. "MAYOR TO FIGHT KLAN LODGE HERE," *Courier-Journal*, Aug. 22, 1921 (ProQuest Historical Newspapers)

542. "MAYOR FORBIDS KLAN MEETING," *Courier-Journal*, Sep. 16, 1921 (ProQuest Historical Newspapers)

543. "SEGREGATION LAW HERE IS HELD INVALID," Nov 6, 1917, *Courier-Journal* (ProQuest Historical Newspapers)

544. "PROTEST TO TENNIS COURTS FOR NEGROES OF NO AVAIL: BOAKD HOLDS THEY HAVE EQUAL RIGHTS IN PARKS," *Courier-Journal*, Sep. 16, 1914 (ProQuest Historical Newspapers).

545. "PROTEST TO TENNIS COURTS FOR NEGROES OF NO AVAIL: BOAKD HOLDS THEY HAVE EQUAL RIGHTS IN PARKS," *Courier-Journal*, Sep. 16, 1914 (ProQuest Historical Newspapers).

546. "President J.B. Castleman Praises Efficiency of Park Board Employes [sic]," *Courier-Journal*, Nov. 9, 1916 (ProQuest Historical Newspapers).

547. "CHICKASAW PARK OPENS IN SPRING," *Courier-Journal*, Feb. 19, 1922 (ProQuest Historical Newspapers). See also "Chickasaw Park," https://louisvilleky.gov/government/parks/park-list/chickasaw-park

548. Letters from 1907-1908, OA Reel 60, LOC

549. Thomas, *Origins*, p. 21.

550. Arleyn A. Levee, *Louisville's Olmsted Park Legacy: Selective Chronology* (Olmsted Parks Conservancy 1992) pp. 57.

551. Kent Masterson Brown, "Double Canister at Ten Yards: Captain Andrew Cowan at Gettysburg," Filson Club History Quarterly, Vol. 59, No. 3, July 1985, p. 293

552. "BEAUTY OF CITY PARKS PRAISED," John B. Castleman and D.F. Murphy, Courier-Journal, Nov. 20, 1917 (ProQuest Historical Newspapers).

553. Letter from Young Allison to Castleman, Feb. 12, 1913, Filson Historical Society

554. Arleyn A. Levee, *Louisville's Olmsted Park Legacy: Selective Chronology* (Olmsted Parks Conservancy 1992) pp. 55.

555. Inventory and Appraisement of Castleman Estate, Sep. 17, 1918, Second Folder, Filson Historical Society.

556. Arleyn A. Levee, *Louisville's Olmsted Park Legacy: Selective Chronology* (Olmsted Parks Conservancy 1992) pp. 58.

557. Rybczynski, *Clearing*, p. 410.

558. Rybczynski, *Clearing*, p. 410.

559. Rybczynski, Clearing, p. 410.

560. Thomas, *Origins*, pp. 221-222.

561. http://www.olmstedparks.org/about/ Several other cities with Olmsted park systems also now have conservancies, which help supplement the local government funds to maintain the park systems in good condition.

ABOUT THE AUTHOR

Eric Burnette, Author

Eric Burnette is a writer with a law degree and a Master's of Urban Planning from the University of Louisville. He lives in Louisville with his wife and two children. They visit the parks frequently.